PRAISE FOR EDWARD JAY EPSTEIN'S
THE BIG PICTURE

"One of the virtues of *The Big Picture* is Mr. Epstein's astonishing access to numbers that the movie studios go to great lengths to keep secret.... [A] groundbreaking work that explains the inner workings of the game."
—The Wall Street Journal

"Illuminating.... Startling.... By the time Epstein is through it's abundantly clear that what we think of as Hollywood is, in accounting terms, a high-stakes hall of mirrors."
—The New York Times

"Edward Jay Epstein is here to tell us that when it comes to Hollywood these days, we've got it all wrong.... Epstein argues, and most persuasively, that we persist in thinking about Hollywood in terms that no longer exist: the 'dream factories' that were the old studios—MGM, RKO, Paramount, Columbia, Fox, Universal and Warner Bros.—where movies were the only products, stars and lesser actors were bound to studios by rigid contracts, and theaters were owned by the studios that supplied them.... [Epstein] is a bulldog researcher, he's brought a great deal of interesting material together and he has interesting things to say."
—Jonathan Yardley, The Washington Post Book World

"In his adroit charting of the confide entities and eras Mr. Epstein kicks u Edward Jay Epstein is quite good."
—Larry McMurtry, The New Review of Books

"Hollywood has needed one of these for a long time—a user's manual. This one could not be more complete. . . . [Grade] A. Keep it in your car... and you'll never get lost in this town again."
—Entertainment Weekly

"I pick no nits with his thesis of a paradigm-dropping shift in the industry."
—William Safire, The New York Times Magazine

"Mr. Epstein rightly describes Hollywood as a close-knit community with a stronger hold on its employees' loyalty than any single company within it."
—The Economist

"...[A] valuable education for those seeking to enter and understand the entertainment industry.... Factually impressive."
—Joel Hirschhorn, Variety

"[*The Big Picture*] fascinatingly describes the evolution of the modern marketing- and brand-driven global media giants.... For anybody who is a film buff, *The Big Picture* will be a fine adventure. But once you learn what goes on behind the scenes, you may never again look at a movie the same way."
—BusinessWeek

"Epstein peels away the Hollywood facade and gives a nuts-and-bolts view of how the six entertainment empires— Viacom, Fox, NBC/Universal, Time Warner, Sony, and Disney—create and distribute intellectual property today.... [He] presents a fascinating look at the unbelievable efforts that must be coordinated to produce a film."
—Booklist

"In vivid detail, he describes the current process of how a film is made, from the initial pitch to last-minute digital editing. There's a refreshing absence of moral grandstanding in Epstein's work. With no apparent ax to grind, he simply and comprehensively presents the industry as it is: the nuts and bolts, the perks and pitfalls and the staggering fortunes that some in the business walk away with. This is the new indispensable text for anyone interested in how Hollywood works."
—Publishers Weekly

"[A] meticulously reported new book."
—The Baltimore Sun

"What one learns from these investigations is that the deepest, darkest secrets in Tinseltown have nothing to do with sex, drugs, blasphemy, or politics, and everything to do with money."
—The Weekly Standard

"Edward Jay Epstein blew the lid off Hollywood's dirty little open secret."
—The Washington Times

"Compelling.... [Epstein] demystifies the contemporary process of film-making in the digital age."
—The Pittsburgh Post-Gazette

ALSO BY EDWARD JAY EPSTEIN

THE
HOLLYWOOD
ECONOMIST

THE
HOLLYWOOD
ECONOMIST

THE HIDDEN FINANCIAL
REALITY BEHIND THE MOVIES

EDWARD JAY EPSTEIN

MELVILLEHOUSE
BROOKLYN, NEW YORK

The Hollywood Economist

© 2010 E.J.E. Publications, Ltd., Inc.

Third Melville House printing: May 2010

Melville House Publishing
145 Plymouth Street
Brooklyn, NY 11201

www.mhpbooks.com

Parts of this book appeared in earlier form in the *New Yorker*, *Slate*, *The Wall Street Journal*, and the *Financial Times*.

Book design by Kelly Blair

Library of Congress Control Number: 2009943414

Printed in the United States of America

For Susana Duncan

CONTENTS

PART III

Hollywood's Invisible Money Machine

PART IV

Hollywood Politics

PART V
The New Studio System

EPILOGUE
The End of the Beginning—Or the End?

APPENDIX

INTRODUCTION

WHY JOURNALISTS DON'T UNDERSTAND HOLLYWOOD

There was a time, around the middle of the twentieth century, when the box office numbers that were reported in newspapers were relevant to the fortunes of Hollywood: studios owned the major theater chains and made virtually all their profits from their theater ticket sales. This was a time before television sets became ubiquitous in American homes, and before movies could be made digital for DVDs and downloads.

Today, Hollywood studios are in a very different business: creating rights that can be licensed, sold, and leveraged over different platforms, including television, DVD, and video games. Box office sales no longer play nearly as important a role. And yet newspapers, as if unable to comprehend the change, continue to breathlessly report these numbers every week, often on their front pages. With few exceptions, this anachronistic ritual is what passes for reporting on the business of Hollywood.

To begin with, these numbers are misleading when used to describe what a film or studio earns. At best, they represent gross income from theater chains' ticket sales. These chains eventually rebate about 50 percent of the sales to a distributor, which also deducts its outlay for prints and advertising (P&A). In 2007, the most recent year for which the studios have released their budget figures, P&A averaged about $40 million per title— more than was typically received from American theaters for a film in that year. The distributor also deducts a distribution fee, usually between 15 and 33 percent of the total theater receipts. Therefore, no matter how well a movie appears to fare in the box office race reported by the media, it is usually in the red at that point.

So where does the money that sustains Hollywood come from? In 2007, the major studios had combined revenues of $42.3 billion, of which about one-tenth came from American theaters; the rest came from the so-called backend, which includes DVD sales, multi-picture output deals with foreign distributors, pay-TV, and network-television licensing.

The only useful thing that the newspaper box office story really provides is bragging rights: Each week, the studio with the top movie can promote it as "Number 1 at the box office." Newspapers themselves are not uninterested parties in this hype: in 2008, studios spent an average of $3.7 million per title placing ads in newspapers. But the real problem with the numbers ritual isn't that it is misleading, but that the focus on it distracts attention from the realities that are reshaping and transforming the movie business. Consider, for example, studio output deals. These arrangements, in which pay-TV, cable networks, and foreign distributors contractually agree to buy an entire slate of future movies from a studio, form a crucial part of Hollywood's cash flow. Indeed, they pay the overhead that allows studios to stay in business. The unwinding of output deals, which started to occur much more frequently in about 2004, can doom an entire studio, as happened in 2008 to New Line Cinema, even though it had produced such immense box office successes as the *Lord of the Rings* trilogy. Yet, despite their importance, output deals are seldom mentioned in the mainstream media. As result, a large part of Hollywood's amazing moneymaking machine remains nearly invisible to the public.

The problem here does not lie in a lack of diligence on the part of the journalists, it proceeds from the entertainment news cycle, which generally requires a story about Hollywood to be linked to an interesting current event within a finite time frame. The ideal example of such an event is the release of a new movie. For such a story, the only readily available data are the weekly box office estimates; these are conveniently reported on websites such as Hollywood.com and Box Office Mojo, which also attach authoritative-sounding demographics to the numbers. If an intrepid reporter decided to pursue a story about the actual profitability of a movie, he or she would need to learn how much the movie cost to make, how much was spent on P&A, the details of its distribution deal and its pre-sales deals abroad, and its real revenues from worldwide theatrical, DVD, television, and licensing income. Such information is far less easily accessible, but it can be found in a film's distribution report. (See, for example, the report on *Midnight in the Garden of Good and Evil* on pages 221-237.) But this report is not sent out to participants until a year after the movie is released, so even if a reporter could obtain it, the newspaper's deadline would be long past. Hence the media's continued fixation on box office numbers, even if reporters are aware of their irrelevance in the digital age.

This book's purpose is to close gaps like these in the understanding of the economic realities behind the new Hollywood. In this pursuit, I benefited enormously from the help I received from people inside the industry. I was greatly aided by distribution reports, budgets, and other documents given to me by producers, directors, and other participants in the making and marketing of movies, and I am deeply indebted to several top studio executives who furnished me with the secret MPA *All Media Revenue Report* for 1998 through 2007 and with studio PowerPoint presentations concerning marketing costs. These documents revealed the global revenue streams of Hollywood films, including the money that flows in from theaters, DVDs, television licensing, and digital downloads.

I am also grateful for the help I received from the Motion Picture Association, which is the major studios' trade and research organization, and particularly from Robert Bauer, its director of strategic planning; Julia Jenks, its director of worldwide research and information analysis; and Dean Garfield, its former executive vice president.

I further thank everyone who answered my often-pesky e-mails (and my sometimes off-the-wall questions), including John Berendt, Jeffrey Bewkes, Laura Bickford, Robert Bookman, Anthony Bregman, Michael Eisner, Bruce Feirstein, Tara Grace, Billy Kimball, Thomas McGrath, Richard Myerson, Edward Pressman, Couper Samuelson, Stephen Schiff, Rob Stone, and Dean Valentine.

I am especially grateful to the very talented director Oliver Stone for casting me in a small part in his *Wall Street 2: Money Never Sleeps* in November 2009. This bit role allowed me to view the art of moviemaking—and it is an art as well as a business—from a perspective that I would not otherwise have had.

I also received an invaluable education in Hollywood law from Alan Rader and Kevin Vick at O'Melveny & Myers, which retained me as an expert witness in the *Sahara* lawsuit, and from Claude

Serra of Weil, Gotshal, and Manges. These lawyers helped me understand the art of the deal.

I also am indebted to those editors who helped shape this material, including Tina Brown and Jeff Frank at *The New Yorker*; Jacob Weisberg and Michael Agger at *Slate*; Howard Dickman, Erich Eichman, and Ray Sokolov at *The Wall Street Journal*; Mario Platero at *Il Sole 24 Ore*; and Gwen Robinson at *The Financial Times*. Finally, I owe a great debt of gratitude to Kelly Burdick at Melville House, who suggested the idea for *The Hollywood Economist*—and brilliantly edited the book.

PART I

THE POPCORN ECONOMY

TEN YEARS AGO, I LEARNED THE REAL SECRET IS THE SALT

Once upon a time, attending the local movie theater was an experience that most Americans shared
on a regular basis. For example, in 1929, the year
of the first Academy Awards, an average of nine-
ty-five million people—about four-fifths of the
ambulatory population—went to movies every
week. There were more than twenty-three thou-

sand theaters, many of palatial size, like the six-thousand-two-hundred-seat Roxy in New York. In those days, the major studios made virtually all the movies that people saw (over seven hundred feature films in 1929). The stars, directors, writers, and other talent were under exclusive contract, and, in addition, the studios owned the theatrical circuits where first-run movies played. This regime, which allowed the major studios to exert total control over movies, from script to screen, came to be known, and feared, as "the studio system"; it more or less ended in 1950, when the United States Supreme Court upheld antitrust decrees ordering several of the major Hollywood studios to divest themselves of their theater chains.

Today, in a world with television, video, the Internet, and other home diversions, weekly average movie attendance is about thirty million, or less than 10 percent of the population. As a result of this diminishment, many larger theaters either closed or divided themselves into smaller auditoriums under one roof. (There are only a third as many theater sites today as there were in 1929, but there are more screens—over thirty thousand.) These multiplexes afforded theater owners significant economies of scale. They could also show a greater variety of films, tailored to different, if smaller, audiences. And as smaller theaters closed the chains expanded; today, the fifteen largest North American chains own approximately two-thirds of all the screens. These large chains, and their centralized film bookers, are the principal gatekeepers for the American film industry. They are responsible for determining what movies most Americans see.

Today a handful of nation-wide multiplex chains account for more than 80 percent of Hollywood's share of the American box office, and a large share of these bookings are done at ShoWest, the annual event in Las Vegas in which movie distribution and exhibition executives meet over four days to discuss plans for releasing and marketing upcoming films. In 1998, I contacted Thomas W. Stephenson, Jr., who then headed one of these major chains, Hollywood Theaters, and arranged to accompany him to ShoWest. Stephenson was willing to let me tag along to meetings in Las Vegas on the condition that I not directly quote or identify those with whom he met. As part of the deal, he agreed to a Don't Ask, Don't Tell protocol in which, unless they specifically asked, he would not identify me as a journalist to the other participants at these meetings with bankers and studio executives.

On the way to Las Vegas, Stephenson, an energetic, peppery-haired man in his early forties, gave me a quick course in the economics of his business. Of the $50 million customers that paid for tickets in 1997, he said his 450-screen chain, Hollywood Theaters, kept only $23 million; most of the rest went to the distributors. But, he continued, since it cost $31.2 million to pay the operating costs of the theaters, his company would have lost $8.2 million if it were limited to the movie-exhibition business. Like all theater owners, though, he has a second business: snack foods, in which the profit margin is well over 80 percent. And with the snack foods, Hollywood Theaters made a profit of $22.4 million on the sale of $26.7 million from its concession stands. "Every element in the lobby," Stephenson told me, "is designed to focus the attention of the customer on its menu boards."

When we arrived, he decided to skip the reception hosted by independent distributors. "I personally enjoy watching many of the low-budget films that come from independents," he said, "but they are not a significant part of our business." In fact, according to Stephenson, 98 percent of the admission revenues of his theater in 1997 came from the principal Hollywood studios—Sony, Disney, Fox, Universal, Paramount, and Warner Bros.

These companies supplied his multiplexes not only with films but with the essential marketing campaigns that accompany them. (Occasionally, to be sure, independent films do succeed in winning a mass audience, as, for example, *The Full Monty* and *Slumdog Millionaire* did; but, as Stephenson put it, "We don't count on them.")

Marketing campaigns begin months before the release date, use the most sophisticated methods available to target demographic groups, and intensify their activity in the final week, often with saturation television advertising, in order to capture "impulse" moviegoers. Stephenson and other theater owners rely on them to muster, if not to create, the audience for a film's crucial opening weekend. The campaigns require massive resources. The major studios spent, on average, $19.2 million in 1997 to advertise each of their films, a sum that would be considerably higher if it included the advertising provided by fast-food restaurants, toy companies, and other retailers in promotional tie-in arrangements that can amount to many times what the studio itself budgets. Rather than attend the large reception, therefore, on our first night we dined with the representative of Coca-Cola, a company that exclusively "pours" the soft drinks in over 70 percent of American movie theaters, including Stephenson's. Soft drinks are an important part of the movie business. All the seats in Stephenson's new theater, and most other multiplexes, are now equipped with their own cup holders, a feature that theater executives consider one of the most groundbreaking innovations in movie-theater history. With cup holders, customers can not only handle drinks more easily in combination with other snacks but can store their drinks while returning to the concession stand for more food. Hollywood Theaters, which now offers an over-sized plastic cup with unlimited refills, sold slightly in excess of $11 million dollars-worth of Coca-Cola products in 1997, of which well over $8 million was profit.

Although most of ShoWest's official functions take place in convention halls and hospitality suites at Bally's Hotel, much unofficial business was done in its sprawling coffee shop. It was there early the next morning that I joined Stephenson for a breakfast meeting with an analyst from J. C. Bradford & Co., an investment firm. Acquisitions were in the air; Kohlberg Kravis Roberts had just bought and consolidated two of the largest theater chains. Stephenson, as he made clear at the outset, planned to partake in this industry consolidation by acquiring state-of-the-art multiplexes. Since he planned to finance this aggressive expansion by selling part of his company to public or private investors, he needed the services of investment bankers who, in turn, needed a story or convincing rationale, to raise the money.

Stephenson's story centered on stadium seating, in which every row of seats is elevated about fourteen inches above the row preceding it, allowing all customers to have an unimpeded view of the screen. While the seats take up more space, Stephenson said, "Our focus groups show that people now seek out theaters with stadium seating and will drive as far as twenty miles to find one that has it." Attendance increased between 30 and 52 percent where he had installed such seating. Stephenson would repeat this story to four other investment bankers at similar kaffeeklatsches over the next two days.

A little later, Stephenson moved to a different table to meet with two of the top executives of another major chain. He had told me beforehand that he wanted to buy five of their multiplexes and sell them an equivalent number in different locations, or "zones." In the movie business, the country is divided into zones that contain anywhere from a few thousand to a few hundred thousand people; the major distributors license their films to only one theater owner in each zone. Just over two-thirds of Stephenson's theaters are in such exclusive zones, and he wanted to increase this number. These talks ended inconclusively, and in the late morning I accompanied Stephenson to the convention hall, where we took assigned seats in the grandstands. Stephenson, along with 3,600 other attendees, was there to see the first major studio presentation, Sony's product reel. Sony's top executives sat on a dais, as if addressing a shareholders' meeting. Jeff Blake, the president of Sony's distribution arm, said that last year Sony films had brought a new record gross into American theaters: $1.2 billion. Indeed, Sony accounted for nearly one out of every four dollars spent on movie tickets in 1997.

Vanna White, the television personality then conducted a mock *Wheel of Fortune* game in which every clue referred to films coming from Sony in the next year, including *Godzilla.* As Vanna White announced each title, actors from the film in question rushed onto the stage—among them such stars as Michelle Pfeiffer, Julia Roberts, Nicolas Cage, and Antonio Banderas. All of this was followed by excerpts from the films. A highlight of sorts came when the stage suddenly filled with dancers costumed as characters from Sony's movies. Robert Goulet played the part of Jeff Blake and sang, to the tune of "The Impossible Dream":

This is our quest, to be king of the box
   There'll be lines round the block
When that big hunk Godzilla is finally here
And you'll know what we've done for
      you lately
When we beat the unbeatable year.

A private meeting held afterward, in Sony's Las Vegas conference room, was far more grounded in reality. A top Sony executive immediately set the tone by observing that the presentation had cost Sony four million dollars (a gross exaggeration, it turned out) and then quipped that next year, instead of hosting the event, Sony would just send a ten-thousand-dollar check to each of the chains' film buyers. It became apparent at this meeting that the negotiations did not concern whether a chain would show Sony films on their prescribed release dates; that was taken for granted. At issue was the terms under which they were to be played and positioned against the films of competing distributors, for instance, the number of screens they would be shown on in a multiplex, the guaranteed length of each film's run, the amount of free advertising there would be in the form of trailers and lobby displays, and the division of the box office receipts.

For example, regarding *Godzilla*, the executive outlined the enormous marketing campaign, supported by worldwide licensees of three thousand *Godzilla* products, as well as promotional tie-ins with such retail partners as Taco Bell, Sprint, Swatch, Hershey's, Duracell, Kirin beer, and Kodak, which were designed to drive a huge and voracious audience of teen-age boys to their theaters. This particular audience, as he described it, was not concerned with the quality of the film, or even whether it was in focus, as long as there was action and popcorn. He joked that the theaters' potential popcorn sales should persuade them to agree to give Sony a larger opening-week cut. Joke or not, the implication was not lost on Stephenson's film buyer, although for the moment he successfully resisted Sony's suggestion. (As it turned out, the *Godzilla* campaign succeeded in "driving" people to pay seventy-four million dollars to see the poorly reviewed lizard in its opening, Memorial Day weekend.)

The next private meeting, in the hospitality suite of Twentieth Century Fox, was more relaxed. After offering Stephenson a soft drink, the Fox executive discussed the strategy for the summer season, which provides the largest audience for theaters. Indeed, of the nearly 1.4 billion tickets sold in 1997, some five hundred million were for the summer season, when, as the Fox executive put it, "Every day is a school holiday." (Another two hundred and thirty million were sold in the so-called holiday season, between Thanksgiving and New Year's.)

For the summer release season, Fox was facing competition from a number of catastrophe films, such as *Godzilla*, *Deep Impact*, and *Armageddon*, which early tracking polls showed were attracting the attention of large numbers of male teens. These polls I saw, which were conducted by the National Research Group, had divided respondents into five demographic "quadrants"— under twenty-five, over twenty-five, male, female, and a racial category—and asked about their awareness of, and interest in, upcoming films. On the basis of these data, along with other research supplied by the company, the major studios can avoid simultaneously competing in the same demographic categories and dividing up their opening-weekend audiences. Even in March, the Fox executive reckoned that competitors' films, particularly *Godzilla* and *Armageddon*, would dominate two crucial quadrants—male and under twenty-five—in the early summer. He therefore opted to counter-program, which meant scheduling romantic comedies, that would appeal to the female and over-twenty-five quadrants.

Although the Fox people had an easier style than their Sony counterparts, they wanted the same limited commodity: the chain's better screens, play dates, and in-theater advertising. So did the four other distributors Stephenson met with during ShoWest. By his count, in four days he watched brief excerpts from some fifty films. "They all tend to blur together," he said, and plots were never described. Instead, the accompanying pitches identified them in such jargon as "Clearasil" (coming-of-age), "genre" (teen-age horror), "romantic comedy" (love story), "ethnic" (black characters), "franchise" (the carbon-copy sequel of another film), and "catastrophe" (volcano, comet/asteroid/monster, loud sound effects). The Holy Grail was a film like *Titanic*, which appealed to all five quadrants. The last and longest meeting was with Disney's distribution arm, Buena Vista; its senior executives were eager to spend an hour or so discussing marketing plans with Stephenson. While they voiced some concern about the proximity of July's *Armageddon*, in which the earth is on a fatal collision path with an asteroid, with Paramount and DreamWorks' *Deep Impact*, in which the world is on a fatal collision path with a comet, they had an ingenious scheme for differentiating their product. Holding up a rectangular box, their executives explained that it contained a kit that would help theater managers to build a mock asteroid. Disney planned to distribute this package to theaters playing *Armageddon* and award prizes to theater managers who used it to create the most forbidding cosmic rock. The theme would then be amplified through such stunts as end-of-the world parties hosted by local disc jockeys.

Later, Stephenson, along with several of his top executives, toured the trade-show pavilions located in two giant tents behind Bally's, where delegates to ShoWest were somewhat greedily sampling popcorn, jelly beans, chocolates, licorice, frankfurters, nachos, and other snacks, many of which claimed innovative new flavors and aromas. Others were getting a look at the non-consumable products at the booths, such as loudspeakers, projectors, ticket rolls, cleaning equipment, marquee letters, plastic cups, and remote ticketing systems.

As we walked around, one of Stephenson's associates stopped to try an oversized Wetzel's pretzel. According to the pretzel company's representative, the Wetzel's, though about three hundred calories, would appeal to diet-conscious non-popcorn-eaters, such as women who wait on the concession line with their boyfriends. At this point, one of Stephenson's top executives, who was assessing different popcorn-topping oil, said to me in a hushed tone that "The real secret is the salt." As a veteran of the movie exhibition business, he explained that the more salt that a movie theater added to the butter it poured over its popcorn, the more money it made since it drove customers back to the concession stand for drinks—where they buy more popcorn. Stephenson concurred, adding, "We are in a very high-margin retail business."

WHY DO MOST NEW MOVIE THEATERS HAVE FEWER THAN 300 SEATS?

The multiplex can be traced back to an otherwise unmemorable shopping center in Kansas City, Missouri in 1963. Its theater owner Stanley H. Durwood split one theater into two "screens," allowing a single box office and concession stand to service audiences watching two different films. In addition, new automated projectors allowed a single untrained (and non-union) projectionist to run an entire program, including trailers, advertisements, and the movie for multiple screens. The arrangement proved so profitable that Durwood's company, American Multi-Cinema, or AMC as it is now known, along with the other major chains, converted most, indeed almost all, of the large movie palaces in America into multiplexes.

What greatly contributed to the shrinking of the multiplex auditoria, or "screens," was the Americans with Disabilities Act (ADA) of 1990. This act requires that new or renovated public theaters with more than 299 seats provide wheelchair access to all rows. Providing such access requires up to one-third more space for the necessary ramps—space that cannot be filled with revenue generating seats. To avoid this problem, multiplex owners divided their space into smaller theaters with a maximum of 299 seats. The result was a further proliferation of screens. Between 1990 and 2005 the total number of screens in the United States rose from 23,000 to nearly 38,000. Since multiplex owners essentially are in the people moving business—moving as many people as possible per hour past their concession stands—they found that the best way that they could maximize this "flow," as one multiplex owner explained, was to show the movies expected to draw the largest audiences on different screens every hour or even half-hour. So the same movies were booked on multiple screens at a single multiplex.

This strategy has recently undermined the studio's system of "zones" and "clearances" in which the studio's distribution arms refuse to provide the same movie to competing theaters in the same locale. This practice made sense in the era of neighborhood movie theaters. Theater owners insisted they needed such protection to prevent audience confusion proceeding from people seeing the same movie playing at two nearby theaters. And studios accommodated even though it meant that they had to have a larger inventory of movies available to make allocations to a larger number of theaters.

This restrictive system became unnecessary when multiplex owners moved towards smaller theaters to deal with the ADA. What multiplexes now wanted were the most heavily advertised new blockbusters even if they were playing across the street (or mall). As Richard Myerson, the general manager of Twentieth Century Fox's distribution arm explained to me, "multiplexes were no longer competing with one another for different movies." They simply wanted to attract a bigger flow of popcorn eaters to their entertainment complex. So as theaters no longer wanted it, the studios happily ended the system.

The consequence of this chain of events is that studios found themselves needing to distribute fewer movies. And this allowed them to further concentrate their resources on producing the action-packed franchise movies that help multiplexes maintain their flow of teen foot traffic past concession stands. Instead of a diverse portfolio of movies, studios could now open a franchise movie such as *Batman Begins, Transformers 2,* or *Spider-Man 3* on 4,000 or more screens and, if successful, get huge grosses flowing through the box offices.

The only down side for studios is that opening on more, smaller screens requires more prints. Back in the 1970s a studio could open a movie with 800 prints (an outlay of $800,000)—even *Star Wars*, the biggest hit of its time, never played on more than 1,100 screens. But with wider openings the cost of prints became far more substantial. With each print costing about $1,500, opening on 4,000 screens requires an outlay of $6 million.

The butterfly effect may even tip the scales in favor of digital projection in the coming decade. After all, if smaller screens continue to replace larger ones because of the ADA challenge, the simplest way that studios have to offset the growing print and distribution cost is to help subsidize a shift in multiplexes from analog to digital projectors. The advantage to studios, as one Paramount executive suggested, is that a studio could open a movie in "30,000 theaters around the world, if only for a weekend," and capture the huge cash-flow that would come from a global campaign. Such a vision, alas, might not bode well for those who enjoy less-action packed non-blockbusters.

SEX IN THE CINEMA: ASSET OR LIABILITY?

In the early days of Hollywood, nudity—or the illusion of it—was considered such an asset that director Cecil B. DeMille famously made bathing scenes an obligatory ingredient of his biblical epics. Nowadays, nudity may be a decided liability when it comes to the commercial success of a movie. The top twenty-five grossing films since 2000—including such franchises as *Spider-Man*, *Lord of The Rings*, *Shrek*, *Harry Potter*, *Batman*, and *The Incredibles*, contained no sexually oriented nudity. In fact, the absence of sex—at least graphic sex—is often key to the success of Hollywood's moneymaking movies since it increases the potential audience of children in both the domestic and foreign markets. To be sure, directors may consider a sex scene artistically integral to their movie, but studios almost always have the right to exercise the final cut, and, if they want to maximize the potential revenue, they have to consider three factors.

First, there is the rating system. For a film to play in movie theaters belonging to the National Association of Theater Owners—which includes all the multiplexes in America—it first needs to obtain a rating from a board organized by the Motion Picture Association of America, the trade association of the six major studios. All the expenses for rating movies are paid to the MPAA by the studio out of a percentage deducted from box office receipts. As it presently works, a movie that contains sexually oriented nudity gets either an NC-17 or an R rating, depending on how graphically sex is depicted. The NC-17 rating, which forbids theaters from admitting children under the age of eighteen, is the equivalent of a death sentence as far as the studios are concerned. In fact, since the financial disaster of Paul Verhoeven's NC-17 *Showgirls* in 1995, no studio has attempted a wide release of a NC-17 film. As one Paramount executive suggested, because of their sexually related nudity, movies such as Louis Malle's *Pretty Baby*, Bernardo Bertolucci's *Last Tango in Paris*, and Stanley Kubrick's *A Clockwork Orange* would not even be considered by a major studio today.

If a movie contains less explicit nudity, it earns an R rating, which merely prohibits youth unaccompanied by an adult. Even though this option means that some number of multiplex employees—who might otherwise be selling popcorn—are required to check the identity documents of the teenage audience, theaters accept R-rated films, as was the case with *Troy*, if the R is for graphic violence because movie violence is a huge attraction for the teen audience. An R rating for nudity has a further problem in the popcorn economy: it greatly complicates the movie's all-important marketing drive. When a film receives an R rating for nudity, many television stations and cable networks, particularly teenage-oriented ones, will not accept TV ads for the movies. In addition, an R rating for nudity will preclude any of the fast-food chains, beverage companies, or toy manufacturers that act as the studios' merchandise tie-in partners from backing the movie with tens of millions of dollars in free advertising. As a result, it becomes much more expensive to alert and herd audiences to theaters for R-rated films.

Second, there is the Wal-Mart consideration. In 2007, the six studios took in $17.9 billion from DVD sales, according to the studios' own internal numbers. Wal-Mart, including its Sam's Club stores, accounted for nearly one-quarter of those sales, which means that Wal-Mart wrote more than $4 billion in checks to the studios in 2007. Such enormous buying power comes dangerously close to constituting what the Justice Department calls a monopsony—control of a market by a single buyer—and it allows the giant retailer to effectively dictate the terms of trade. While Wal-Mart may not use its clout to advance any political agenda or social engineering objective, Wal-Mart does use DVDs to lure in customers who, while they pass through the store, may buy more profitable items, such as toys, clothing, or electronics. For this task, Wal-Mart's concern with the content of DVDs is that they not offend important customers—especially mothers—by containing material that may be inappropriate for children. Hence its "decency policy" that consigns DVDs containing sexually related nudity to "adult sections" of the store, which greatly reduces their sales. (Wal-Mart is less concerned with vulgar behavior and language.) These guidelines, in turn, put studios under tremendous pressure to sanitize their films of nudity.

Finally, movies with nudity are a problem for the studios' other main moneymaker: television. As became abundantly clear in the controversy surrounding Janet Jackson's wardrobe malfunction at Super Bowl XXXVIII, broadcast television is a government-regulated enterprise. When the government grants a free license to a station to broad-cast over the public airwaves, it does so under the condition that it conform to the rules enforced by the Federal Communications Commission. Among those rules is the standard of "public decency," which among other things specifically prohibits salacious nudity, which is why CBS had to pay a fine for Ms. Jackson's brief exposure. Because the FCC regulates broadcast television (though not cable television), television stations run similar risks and embarrassments—if they show movies that include even partially nudity.

So, before a studio can license such a movie to a broadcast network, it first has to cut out all the nudity and other scenes that run afoul of the de-cency standard. Aside from the expense involved, it requires the hassle of obtaining the director's permission, which is contractually required by the Directors Guild of America. The same is true in studio sales to foreign television companies, which have their own government censorship.

Since graphic sex in movies is a triple liability, the studios can be expected to increasingly find that the artistic gain that comes from including it does not compensate for the financial pain and green-light fewer and fewer movies that present this problem. We may live in an anything-goes age, but if a studio wants to make money, it has to limit how much of "anything"—at least anything sexually explicit—it shows on the big screen. As one studio executive with an MBA lamented, "We may have to leave sex to the independents." In the New Hollywood, as far as studios are concerned, no nudes is good news.

THE VANISHING BOX OFFICE

The regular movie audience has been so decimated over the past six decades that the habitual weekly adult moviegoer will soon qualify, if not as an endangered species, as a niche group. In 1948, 65 percent of the population went to a movie house in an average week; in 2008, under 6 percent of the population went to see a movie in an average week. What changed in the interval was that virtually every American family bought a TV set. In 1948, when home TV was still a rarity, theaters sold 4.6 billion tickets. By 1958, TV had penetrated most American homes, and theaters sold only 2 billion tickets. The Hollywood studios tried to counter television with technology dazzle, including wider screens (CinemaScope), noisier speakers (surround sound), and more visually exciting special effects, but technology did nothing to stem the mass defections. They also tried epic, three-hour movies, such as *Ben Hur*, *Lawrence of Arabia*, and *Dr. Zhivago*, that, although they succeeded individually, had little effect on the weekly movie audience. Even the much-heralded fantasy bonanzas of Spielberg and Lucas could not halt the decline. By 1988, ticket sales hovered at 1 billion. The studios, realizing that they could no longer count on habitual moviegoers to fill theaters, devised a new strategy: creating audiences de novo for each movie via paid advertising.

Audience-creation is a very expensive enterprise—in 2007 the studios' average cost for advertising a film was $35.9 million. Studios justified this expenditure on the grounds that huge opening-weekend audiences would help turn a movie into an "event," generating word-of-mouth and other free advertising that would continue to bring moviegoers into theaters, and, later, into video stores. *Titanic*, for example, took in only a modest $28 million over its opening weekend. Two weeks later, after it had become a word-of-mouth event, the movie had earned $149 million. It wound up grossing a phenomenal $600 million at American theaters. While no other film has equaled the success of *Titanic*, such "event" films are what studios depend upon to pay the bills.

What terrifies top studio executives now is the dearth of word-of-mouth event movies. "Word of mouth is no longer a factor," Thomas McGrath, a former Paramount vice president explained. Instead, studio marketing chiefs try for big opening numbers by driving with a drumbeat of TV ads the one audience they can rely on: male teens. While with $36 million of ads they can still manufacture weekend teen audiences, they can no longer create the event movies that the studios need. Meanwhile, a quantum leap in quality in high-definition DVDs, television sets, and digital recorders threatens to further erode the edge movie theaters have over home entertainment. Studio executives are coming to grip with the reality that they have as much chance of reversing the secular shift of audiences from the theater to the home as King Canute had in commanding the tide to recede.

But what alternative do they have? The skill that movie executives have honed over the years is audience-creation. Even if it takes $30 to 50 million to herd teens to the multiplexes, and the movie fails to earn back that outlay, they hope it will lead to a future franchise. To abandon that hope means the end of Hollywood, as they know it.

THE REEL SILVER LINING

The public most often sees Hollywood through the lens of paparazzi cameras and the PR wires of publicists as a wildly extravagant, if not recklessly wasteful, place from which stars, accompanied by personal entourages, fly to lavish parties in private jets. But there is a less profligate side to Hollywood: the culture of the suits, in which the tight-fisted executives who run the studios pride themselves on their ability to pinch pennies out of movie budgets and wring profits out of unlikely places. Consider, for example, the profits studios found in their graveyards of dead prints. Up until the mid-1980s the initial opening of a movie required only several hundred prints—*Star Wars*, for example, opened in 1977 on only thirty-two screens. Nowadays, with simultaneous global openings, it takes 5,000 to 10,000 prints to open major movies. The 2009 sequel in Warner Bros.' Batman franchise, *The Dark Knight*, for example, which played on over 9,000 screens in the US alone, required 12,000 prints for its worldwide distribution, each costing about $1,500. Studios order the prints for these immense runs from film labs and then deduct their cost from the first revenues that flow in from the theaters. So the film production company, which is almost always set up as a separate business entity, absorbs the cost on its books. Then after a brief shelf life of a few weeks in the multiplexes, almost all the prints—except for a few hundred sent to theaters on military bases—are scrapped.

But studios found in this mounting scrap heap a literal silver lining. Each shredded print contains a small quantity of silver, which the studios can "mine" via a recovery process and sell. Silver mining, to be sure, is not a new pursuit in Hollywood. Much of the studios' pre-1950s libraries, including many of the irreplaceable negatives of its classics, were destroyed to recover the silver. But with rising precious metal prices—silver exceeded $18 an ounce on the commodity market in November 2009—and hundreds of thousands of dead prints to mine, it provides a rich vein of extra income for the studios (which is not returned to the film production companies charged for the prints). Of course, this mine will peter out as more and more multiplexes convert from analog to digital projection, and prints themselves are no longer necessary.

Even though the proceeds studios recover from prints may amount to little more than "pocket money," as a Paramount executive described it, it fulfills a vital requisite for the suit culture: finding new sources of income.

PART II

STAR CULTURE

THE CONTRACT'S THE THING—
IF NOT FOR HAMLET, FOR ARNOLD
SCHWARZENEGGER

The nonstop anecdotes that stars give in celebrity interviews about the stunts they supposedly performed, their favorite hobbies, and how much they enjoyed working with other stars may serve to hype their latest project—a job they are contractually required to do—but they evade a central issue: the art of the deal has come to replace the art of movies. To understand how the new Hollywood really works, one need only read stars' contracts. Consider, for example, Governor Arnold Schwarzenegger's agreement for *Terminator 3: The Rise of the Machines*. It's a state-of-the-art exercise in deal-making.

The contract was brilliantly put together by the Hollywood super-lawyer Jacob Bloom between June 2000 and December 2001, requiring no fewer than twenty-one drafts, and runs thirty-three pages (including appendices). For starters, Schwarzenegger got a $29.25 million "pay or play" fee, meaning he would be paid whether or not the movie was made. (At the time, that figure was a record for guaranteed compensation.) The first $3 million would be delivered on signing and the balance during the course of nineteen weeks of "principal photography," which is the part of a production during which the actors are in front of the camera. For every week the shooting ran over its nineteen-week schedule, Schwarzenegger would receive an additional $1.6 million in "overage." Then there was the "perk package"—a lump sum of $1.5 million for private jets, a fully equipped gym trailer, three-bedroom deluxe suites on locations, round-the-clock limousines, and personal bodyguards. The producers Mario Kassar and Andrew Vajna did not agree to pay Schwarzenegger this record sum because he possessed unique acting skills—after all, the part he was to play (along with a digital double and many stuntmen) was that of a slow-speaking robot. They also did not pay Schwarzenegger on the basis of his box office track record. Indeed, his previous two films, *End of Days* (1999) and *The Sixth Day* (2000), had failed both at the world box office and at video rental stores. Nevertheless, in the ten years that had elapsed since *Terminator 2: Judgment Day*, Schwarzenegger's image had become so inexorably linked in video games and TV reruns to the deadly robot that he had become the crucial element of the deal and Kassar and Vajna needed him to raise money.

To make this deal Kassar and Vajna first needed to get the rights to the moribund franchise. So, backed by the German-owned movie financier Intermedia Films, they bought the sequel rights to the *Terminator* franchise for $14.5 million from the bankrupt Carolco Pictures and the initial producer, Gale Anne Hurd. Next, they spent another $5.2 million developing a script. That was the easy part. Now they needed $160 million in financing, which was more than any other movie had cost in those days. They had lined up three distributors: Warner

Bros. would pay $51.6 million for North American rights, the Tokyo distributor Toho-Towa would pay $20 million for Japanese rights, and Sony Pictures Entertainment would pay $77.4 million for the rest of the world. (The balance would come mainly from tax shelter deals in Germany.) But all three distributors—Warner Bros., Sony, and Toho-Towa—made their financing conditional on Schwarzenegger signing on to play the robot. So: No Schwarzenegger, no money.

Kassar and Vajna had no real choice but to accept Schwarzenegger's terms if they wanted to make the movie (and, aside from reviving the franchise, they themselves would earn $10 million in producer fees if the deal went through). Schwarzenegger's demands, however, did not stop with the guarantee of $29.25 million. He also insisted on and got 20 percent of the gross receipts made by the venture from every market in the world—including movie theaters, videos, DVDs, television licensing, in-flight entertainment, game licensing, and so forth—once the movie had reached its cash breakeven point. Such "contingent compensation" is not unusual in movie contracts, but, in some cases, Hollywood accounting famously uses smoke and mirrors to make sure to define "breakeven" in such a way that a movie never reaches it. Schwarzenegger's contract, thanks to the ingenious lawyering of Jake Bloom, allowed for no such evasion.

Schwarzenegger also could decide who worked with him. The contract "pre-approval" clause gave him choice of not only the director (Jonathan Mostow) and the principal cast, but also his hairdresser (Peter Toothbal), his makeup man (Jeff Dawn), his driver (Howard Valesco), his stand-in (Dieter Rauter), his stunt double (Billy Lucas), the unit publicist (Sheryl Merin), his personal physician (Dr. Graham Waring), and his cook (Steve Hunter). Finally, Schwarzenegger had the contract structured to give him every possible tax advantage.

All the money was to be paid not to Schwarzenegger but to Oak Productions Inc., a corporate front he controlled. Oak Productions, in return, "lends" Schwarzenegger's services to the production. Since Schwarzenegger didn't get any money personally from the movie itself, he had more flexibility managing his exposure to taxes. For example, Oak Productions entered into a complex tax-reimbursement scheme with the production to help avoid additional tax liabilities that might occur abroad. In return, Schwarzenegger agreed to make himself available for eighteen weeks of principal photography, one week (on a nonexclusive basis) for rehearsals—if any were required—and five days for re-shooting. In addition, he had to make himself available for at least ten days, seven of them abroad, for promotional activities in connection with the initial theatrical release of the movie. This media work included everything from television and radio appearances to appearances at premieres and Internet chat rooms. The negotiation of this contract did not come cheaply—the legal and accounting budget for the movie was $2 million—and, by the time all of Schwarzenegger's demands were met, the budget of the film had risen to $187.3 million, making it then the most expensive independently produced movie in history. Another $90 million was spent advertising and marketing it.

Terminator 3 had a world box office gross of $433 million which, together with DVD, TV, and other rights, allowed the distributors to eke out a small profit, but Arnold Schwarzenegger, who had created his own "cash breakeven," was the big winner. In the bygone days of the studio system, the studios had exclusive contracts with their stars that allowed them to reap the profits from the images their PR machines had created. In the new Hollywood, the stars themselves reap the profit their brand names bring to a film. So it is not surprising that even after Schwarzenegger became the governor of California in 2004, his holding company protected his image rights by suing a small toy maker selling a Schwarzenegger-like bobble-head doll on the grounds that "Schwarzenegger is an instantly recognizable global celebrity whose name and likeness are worth millions of dollars and are solely his property."

Ironically, whereas Schwarzenegger was crucial to making the deal, once the *Terminator* franchise had been successfully resurrected, his acting services were no longer necessary for future sequels. In 2007, Kassar and Vajna sold the rights to the franchise to the game company Halycon for $25 million, which produced *Terminator Salvation* in 2009, the first of three planned sequels. Even without Schwarzenegger, who was by now fighting his own budget battles as governor of California, it did almost as well as *Terminator 3* at the domestic box office, though not as well in the Asian markets.

MOVIE STARS COME IN TWO FLAVORS: $20 MILLION AND FREE

The difference between studio-made movies and independent-made movies is the former have an American distributor before they are filmed, or even green-lit, and therefore investors in them are assured that they will be shown in theaters, while the latter don't. And since it may take years of screenings, and endless trips to film festivals, before an indie film has a chance of finding an American distributor and many never do, raising money for them is a daunting challenge.

One ingenious device through which indie film producers overcome this problem is to recruit Hollywood stars who will work for them on the cheap and use their names to pre-sell the movie abroad. The same actors and actresses who quote Hollywood studios $20 million per movie will work on indie films for a small fraction of that fee. Often they accept "scale," as the Screen Actors Guild's minimum wage of $788 a day is called, or "near scale" of about $10,000 a week plus overtime. Instead of requiring private jets, luxury suites, and multimillion dollar perk packages as they do in studio films, the stars will fly on commercial flights, stay in inexpensive condos, and get the same per diem as the rest of the cast. Instead of receiving a sizable chunk of the gross receipts as they are accustomed to on studio films, for indie films stars will accept "net points" (even though they—or their agents—are no doubt familiar with David Mamet's famous observation that in Hollywood, "There is no Net"). "The total cost of a star can be less than that of running the office Xerox," explained one knowledgeable producer. The willingness of top stars—including Keanu Reeves, Mel Gibson, Jim Carrey, Will Ferrell, Drew Barrymore, Al Pacino, Angelina Jolie, Pierce Brosnan, Leonardo DiCaprio, Charlize Theron, Tobey Maguire, Demi Moore, Sean Penn, and Julia Roberts—to work for near scale in the parallel universe of indie films allows indie producers to take advantage of a star's cachet to finance the movies.

Ironically, in the era of the moguls, the Hollywood studios gained a similar advantage over stars by locking all their actors and actresses into long-term contracts in which they were paid a specified weekly salary regardless of the success of their movies. After the studio system collapsed in the late 1940s, the stars, represented by powerful talent agencies, quickly turned the tables on the studios. Now, no longer under studio contract, the stars auctioned off their services to the highest bidder from film to film. The studios still paid for their films' publicity, but the stars now reaped the benefits of their cachet via product endorsement, licensing their images for games and toys, and a raft of other celebritized enterprises.

Despite the lure of enormous compensation from studios, which now include perk packages and cuts of the gross receipts that can easily exceed $30 million a film, stars find occasional satisfaction in working for coolie wages in indie productions, making a distinction between, as one top Creative Artists Agency (CAA) agent put it, "commerce and art." Some stars may find that roles in studio comic-book movies (that they share with live stuntmen and digital doubles) do not provide the acting opportunities, award possibilities, prestige, camaraderie, or even aura of coolness of indie productions. Others may want to work with a particular director, such as Woody Allen, Spike Jonze, or David Mamet, or burnish their fading image as an actor. They might also need to fill a hole in their schedule since, PR hype aside, there is not an endless cornucopia of $20 million parts in Hollywood. Also, when stars do "artistic" films practically pro bono they do not officially lower their $20 million quote.

Whatever the star's motives, the indie producers get, if not a free ride, a means of financing their movies through a three-step process called pre-sales. Here is how it works:

Step One. The indie producer makes a pre-sale contract with a distributor overseas. In such an arrangement, the producer usually turns over all rights to exhibit the movie—including selling

DVDs and TV licenses—in a particular country in return for a minimum guarantee of money once the film is completed and delivered. The catch-22 here is that a foreign distributor often will not commit to a pre-sale contract if there is no American distributor or unless the film has a recognizable star (with a star the distributor has at least a chance of selling the DVD and TV rights). So indie producers must persuade or seduce a star into joining the movie—and here is where the genius comes in—for practically no money. With a star in tow, a producer can often make enough pre-sales to cover most, if not all, of the budget.

Step Two. Since pre-sales are no more than promissory notes, the indie producer must borrow against them from banks to pay for the movie. Before he can do that, he needs to guarantee the banks that the movie, once begun, will get finished and delivered to foreign distributors. What's needed is a completion bond, which guarantees the banks that it will pay all cost overruns necessary to finish the movie and if the production is abandoned, it will pay all the money lost on the venture, which means that one way or another the bank will get back its money. Two companies, Film Finance, Inc. and International Film Guarantors, provide almost all the completion bonds for independent productions. (Studios that internally finance their own movies do not need completion bonds.) Before either company will sell a producer a completion bond, the producer has to meet its requisites, which include buying full insurance for the star (so if he or she is injured or quits the completion bond coverer gets all the money back from the insurer) and turning over to the completion bond company the ultimate control of the budget (including the right, if anything goes wrong, to take over the production and bring in its own director to complete it). The indie producer also has to pay the company about 2 percent of the budget.

Step Three. With the completion bond in hand, and the pre-sales contracts as collateral, the producer then borrows the money from a bank or other financier. Since the completion bond companies are themselves backed by giant insurers, such as Lloyds of London and Fireman's Fund, the banks take only a very limited risk in making such loans. John W. Miller, who recently retired as head of JP Morgan Chase's movie financing unit, told me that in issuing billions of dollars in loans he did not read the scripts of the indie films he finances. "My bet is on the solvency of the distributors." When these pre-sales contracts are with established international distributors, such as Sony

Pictures, Canal Plus, Toho Films, or Buena Vista International, that risk is, he said "negligible."

Even after scaling all these hurdles, securing the money, and making the movie, the indie producer faces one further challenge: getting the movie into American multiplexes. Even with a completed movie and star, finding a distributor requires going from film festival to film festival, an odyssey that often proves unfruitful. (More than 2,000 indie films were submitted to the Sundance Film Festival in 2009, for example, of which about one percent were accepted.) However, the presence of a star greatly improve its chances, especially in those festivals, such as Cannes, Berlin, Venice, and Toronto, that depend on stars for publicity and photo-ops. As one highly successful indie producer explains, it gives the acquisition executives there more of an incentive to give the film a chance with distribution, because they figure that, even if the film is a hard sell, they can always promote the star. Selling the film ultimately is what it's all about. So the Hollywood star as *homo ludens*, or at least seeking some kind of non-monetary gratification, winds up as the crucial element in a business model that has sustained a large part of independent films—and, for that, we can all be grateful.

THE ANGST QUESTION IN HOLLYWOOD: WHAT IS YOUR CASH BREAKEVEN?

In the arcane universe of Hollywood contracts, there are two kinds of money paid to stars, directors, actors, and other participants in movies. The first kind is called "fixed compensation" and is paid out, like any other wage, when the participant does his job. The second kind is called "contingent compensation," which depends on how well the film does, is typically not paid until the revenues reach an arbitrary point artfully called "cash breakeven" Whatever percentage a participant is supposed to get, whether it is based on gross or net points, it is triggered by this contractual definition. In some contracts in lieu of the star receiving any sizable fixed compensation, the cash breakeven is set at dollar one, which means his pay kicks in immediately after the print and advertising costs are reimbursed, but usually it is set high enough to allow a studio to recover most of its production costs. Not only may the definition vary from film to film, but it is not unusual for many participants in the same film to have different cash breakevens. For each participant it is defined not by any set accounting rules but by Hollywood's prevailing Golden rule: Who has the gold makes the rules. The contentious negotiations, which center around self-serving claims about how much gold any participant might add to the venture, almost irresistibly lead to the most powerful player getting the lowest cash breakeven, which means he or she will be the first to get paid. The problem here is that the money paid first to the more powerful players is added to the cost side of the equation for everyone else, which pushes them further away from reaching their higher cash breakeven. As a result, the less powerful, which includes writers, may never qualify for their contingency payments. Woody Allen jokes in his movie *Hollywood Ending* about a director being so lowly regarded that he received "quadruple cash breakeven," and therefore the movie had to gross four times his breakeven point before he received a penny of his contingency pay. On the other hand, the handful of stars and directors who are indispensable to a movie getting green-lighted can dictate their own golden cash breakeven. And, to protect the egos of less privileged participants in the Hollywood Community, these golden cash breakevens are usually kept a closely guarded secret. But consider the golden terms Arnold Schwarzenegger got for *Terminator 3*. Brilliantly drafted by his lawyer, his cash breakeven clause specifies:

> Cash Breakeven shall be defined as the point at which there shall have been re-

couped from Adjusted Gross Receipts an amount equaling all actual distribution expenses attributable to the Picture (provided there shall be no double deductions for any item, including without limitation residuals), all costs of production of the Picture (including without limitation any pre-break participations, mutually-approved deferments and completion bond fee), actual interest and actual financing costs related to the Picture, a producer fee in the aggregate amount of $5,000,000 for Andy Vajna and Mario Kassar and an overhead charge to Intermedia Film Equities Limited equal to ten percent (10 percent) of the bonded budget (with no interest on overhead or overhead on interest). For purposes of calculating Cash Breakeven only, Adjusted Gross Receipts shall include a 100 percent home video royalty (i.e. home video revenues less costs, provided no such costs shall be deducted if such costs were previously deducted hereunder) to the extent that Producer is accounted by distributors at a 100 percent home video royalty or if Producer is not accounted for at a 100 percent home video royalty, with respect to any Adjusted Gross Receipts, such Adjusted Gross Receipts shall include and be calculated with a home video royalty equal to the home video royalty Producer receives with respect to such Adjusted Gross Receipts, but in no event less than a 35 percent home video royalty. For all other purposes (other than calculating Cash Breakeven), including the calculation of [Schwarzenegger] Participation and the Deferred Participation, Adjusted Gross Receipts shall include a 35 percent home video royalty, or if the agreement for the services of the director of the Picture so provides, then such greater home video royalty shall be included in the Adjusted Gross Receipts of the Picture for purposes of calculating [Schwarzenegger] Participation and the Deferred Participation.

Take video and DVD sales, for example. Under the standard Hollywood contract, studios credit the film with a video "royalty" equal only to 20 percent of the sales. That means that if sales of a DVD total $20 million, only $4 million of that is

100 Days MAIN UNIT PHOTOGRAPHY | Commence Pre-Production: Nov 19th
63 Loc L.A/37 LA Stage/ | Commence Photography: April 15
RECEIVED | Answer Print: April 1St, 2003 S?
60 DAYS SECOND UNIT | Post Production: 27 Weeks | DRAFT - CONFIDENTIAL
45 Days Full
15 Reduced | File: T3 Master Budget Friday,
7 DAYS AERIAL UNIT | CRITICAL ASSUMPTION- LAST ...
Prepared: Feb 12, 2002 | OF SHOOTING ARE ON STAGES

Acct#	Category Title	Page	Total
1100	STORY & RIGHTS	1	$19,569,305
1200	PRODUCER & STAFF	1	$10,022,210
1300	DIRECTOR & STAFF	4	$5,006,294
1400	TALENT	5	$34,565,246
1500	ATL TRAVEL & LIVING	19	$0
1900	TOTAL ATL FRINGES		$1,312,846
	Total Above-The-Line		$70,476,901
2000	PRODUCTION STAFF	19	$1,964,396
2100	EXTRA TALENT	28	$395,803
2200	ART DEPARTMENT	29	$1,613,334
2300	SET CONSTRUCTION	37	$6,954,815
2500	SET OPERATIONS	45	$2,820,579
2600	SPECIAL EFFECTS	53	$4,494,422
2700	SET DRESSING	57	$2,422,254
2800	ACTION PROPS	62	$776,818
00	WARDROBE	64	$1,636,379
000	PICT. VEH. & ANIMALS	68	$1,478,725
3100	MAKEUP & HAIR	72	$555,812
3200	ELECTRICAL	74	$2,578,571
3300	CAMERA	77	$2,419,866
3400	SOUND	82	$358,865
3500	TRANSPORTATION	84	$3,953,281
3600	LOCATION	100	$4,361,743
3700	FILM & LAB	111	$1,035,505
3800	VIDEO TAPE	112	$184,498
3900	CREATURE EFFECTS	113	$3,166,000
4000	FACILITY EXPENSES	114	$1,877,450
4100	TESTS	114	$60,000
4200	SECOND UNIT	115	$5,148,117
4300	AERIAL UNIT	136	$256,751
4400	SPECIAL PHOTOGRAPHY	139	$316,091
4500	COMPUTER GRAPHICS	139	$203,793
4900	TOTAL BTL FRINGES		$6,509,473
	Total Production		$57,446,342
5000	EDITING & PROJECTION	141	$2,512,563
5100	VIDEO TAPE POST	146	$288,552
5200	MUSIC	149	$1,836,154
5300	SOUND (POST PRODUCTION)	150	$691,493
5400	VISUAL EFFECTS	152	$19,889,050
5600	FILM, TAPE, & LIBRARY	154	$301,683
00	TITLES & OPTICALS	155	$142,500
00	TOTAL POST FRINGES		$584,682
	Total Post Production		$26,047,087
6500	PUBLICITY	155	$141,500
6700	INSURANCE	156	
00	GENERAL EXPENSES	156	$2,000,000
00	COMPLETION BOND FEE		$1,796,151
7000	CONTINGENCY		$2,382,585
7300	TOTAL OTHER FRINGES		$7,000,000
	Total Other		$30,668
	TOTAL ABOVE-THE-LINE		$13,360,904
	TOTAL BELOW-THE-LINE		$70,476,901
	TOTAL ABOVE & BELOW-THE-LINE		$96,844,333
	GRAND TOTAL		$167,320,233
			$187,320,233

Where does Hollywood's money go? See the budget for
Terminator 3 above. The internal breakdown of this budget
is over 100 pages.

counted toward reaching the breakeven point. In the case of DVD and video royalties, the contract specifies: "For purposes of calculating Cash Breakeven only, Adjusted Gross Receipts shall include a 100 percent home video royalty (i.e. home video revenues less costs)." So unlike weaker players, Schwarzenegger could count all the money taken in from DVDs and video, $20 million, less their actual cost, toward reaching the threshold where he gets his cut. Of course these payments to Schwarzenegger effectively came at the expense of less powerful talent (like writers) with higher breakeven points. But that is part of the contract game.

THE SAD LESSON OF NICOLE KIDMAN'S KNEE—OR WHAT A STAR NEEDS TO GET A PART

A star must be insurable. Cast insurance is the sine qua non for a movie to be financed. A production company cannot get a completion bond, which financing institutions insist on, unless it has insurance coverage for the star, especially if the star is deemed an "essential element" of the film. With it, if the star dies, becomes disabled or ill, refuses to perform, or abandons the film, the insurer agrees to cover the resulting loss—which may be the entire investment in the project. For example, if anything had happened to Arnold Schwarzenegger in *Terminator 3*, the insurers would have had to pay in excess of $150 million. (The insurance for *Terminator 3* was $2 million.)

For their part, insurers attempt to reduce their exposure to disaster by deciding whom not to insure. They not only evaluate the past history and claim pattern of stars, but they require many levels of medical examination and drug sampling before and during shooting. They may also place restrictions on activities—such as stunts—and assign "watchers" on the set to make sure that stars honor those restrictions. If stars present too great a risk, insurers can elect either to make the premiums prohibitively high or to refuse to insure them altogether.

Nicole Kidman is a case in point. Kidman injured her knee during the filming of *Moulin Rouge* in Australia in 2000, resulting in a $3-million insurance loss, and then quit *Panic Room* in 2001, leading to the insurer having to pay some $7 million for the replacement actress (Jodie Foster). As a result, her public and critical acclaim notwithstanding, Miramax was initially unable to get insurance on her for its film *Cold Mountain*, which had a budget approaching $100 million. From the perspective of the insurer, Fireman's Fund, she was a definite risk. As an insurance executive noted in an email, "While the doctors who did her surgery and her current knee doctor can say she is fully recovered, the fact remains that the doctor we sent her to for her examination noted swelling in the knee." The executive goes on: "The other major fact that can't be changed is our paying three claims for this actress's knees over the years."

To get the necessary policy from Fireman's Fund, Kidman agreed to put $1 million of her own salary in an escrow account that would be forfeited if she failed to maintain the production schedule, and she agreed to use a stunt double for all scenes that the insurer considered potentially threatening to her knee. In addition, the co-producer, Lakeshore Entertainment, added another $500,000 to the escrow account. Only after the completion-bond company, International Film Guarantors, certified that "Kidman is fully aware that she must get through this picture without a problem," adding, "She fully understands this and will not allow anything to get in the way of her finishing this picture"—did she get her insurance—and her role in *Cold Mountain*. Having made the all-important move from borderline uninsurable to borderline insurable, she could make movies again. No matter how great their acting skills and box office drawing power, stars cannot get lead roles if they are uninsurable. Great acting skills and box office drawing power may make the star, but insurance is what it takes to make the movie.

THE STARLET'S DILEMMA

"Everything's geared to fifteen-year-olds... I have girlfriends who are twenty-five in L.A. who are lying about their age because people tell them they're too old. That's how pathetic it is."
   —Morgan Fairchild

In Hollywood, where the radioactive half-life of a starlet's fame may be briefer than her high school education, the effective career of an actress can be nasty, brutish, and short, or, in the lingo, "way harsh." The opportunities for a pretty starlet in the romantic comedies, horror films, and the amusement-park films that are made for the Clearasil crowd tend to dry up when they hit thirty, one of Hollywood's most insightful producers told me. They have to start acting "as opposed to simply gracing the screen with their gorgeous presence and many of those starlets are just not equipped for this second step." Anti-aging camouflage, such as plastic surgery, Botox, collagen injections,

and other elixirs may provide a brief respite but
eventually every actress comes up against the age
stereotyping in Hollywood famously described
by Goldie Hawn: There are only three ages for
women: Babe, District Attorney, and *Driving
Miss Daisy*. Some actresses succeed in breaking
through this age barrier but even they find it a
daunting challenge to escape Hollywood's requisite and satisfy the youth culture, as Rosanna Ar-
quette demonstrates in her interviews with Meg
Ryan, Holly Hunter, Charlotte Rampling, Sharon
Stone, Whoopi Goldberg, Martha Plimpton, and
a score of other actresses in her 2002 documentary *Searching For Debra Winger*. Equally illuminating
are Nancy Ellison's photographs in *Starlets: Before
They Were Famous* of gorgeously posed actresses
who, having failed to make it through the Babe
portal, vanished from Hollywood. As Martha
Plimpton explains about casting, "It's either, she's
a starlet or she's an old hag." Such ageism proceeds not from malice, ignorance, or disdain for
the performers on the part of studio executives,
but from their business model.

When studios found that they could no longer
count on habitual moviegoers to fill theaters, they
went into the very risky business of creating tailor-made audiences for each and every movie they
released. Like in an election campaign, the studios

had to get people to turn out at the multiplexes on a specific date—the opening weekend. The principal means of generating this audience is to buy ads on national television. For this strategy to work efficiently, the studios find a target audience that predictably clusters around programs on which they can afford to buy time. They then bombard this audience—usually seven times in the preceding week to an opening—with thirty-second eye-catching ads.

The studios zero in on teens not because they necessarily like them, or even because the teens buy buckets of popcorn, but because they are the only demographic group that can be easily motivated to leave their home. Even though lassoing this teen herd is enormously expensive—over $30 million a film—the studios profit from the fact that this young audience is also the coin of the realm for merchandisers such as McDonald's, Domino's, and Pepsi. The studios depend upon these companies for tie-deals that can add a hundred million dollars or more in advertising to a single film and can expand the primary audience for DVDs, video games, and other licensable properties on which the studios now bank on for their economic survival. Studios therefore place the lion's share of their TV advertising—over 80

percent in 2005—on the cable and network programs that are watched primarily by people under
twenty-five. The studios also incorporate music in
their sound tracks that teenagers listen to, and try
to cast the sort of babe-actresses that their crucial audience can relate to, if not fantasize about.
Adrienne Shelley, the star of *The Unbelievable Truth*,
for example, described her casting experience this
way: "I get a call in my car on the way to an audi-
tion from the agent. He said, 'What is really important is that they think you are fuckable.'"

Of course, for the ex-babe actress who is no
longer able or willing to play this Hollywood game,
there is always the possibility of starring in foreign
and independent movies, especially if her name
helps raise money abroad. But while roles in these
more adult-oriented movies may be more artistically
rewarding than roles as fantasy-bait in teen movies,
they are rarely, if ever, as high-paying.

THERE IS NO NET

Unlike the dozen or so powerful star actors, directors and producers, such as Tom Cruise, Steven Spielberg, and Jerry Bruckheimer, who get a
cut of the gross revenue of a movie, regardless

of whether the movie is in the red or black, most creative people who produce, write, direct, or act in movies get, in addition to their up front fees, a percentage of the net profits, called "net points." No matter how much the movie seems to take in at the box office, these so-called "net players" rarely ever see a penny from their net points. The frustration that runs rife in Hollywood social circles is summed up in David Mamet's *Speed-the-Plow* when the lead character says that what he has learned about the movie business is "There is no net!"

The reason net players realize little more than psychic income from their "points" is that studios set up each movie as a separate off-the-books corporation designed to produce revenue for the gross players, which include the studio itself since it takes a dollar-one distribution fee of up to 30 percent of the gross and an overhead fee of fifteen percent gross; equity partners who often are given direct cuts, called "corridors," into discreet portions of the gross, and offset their financial risks; and any stars who are gross players. After these cuts, and the costs and interest (10 percent per annum) are deducted, there rarely is anything in the net pie.

Consider, for example, what happened with the revenue from Disney's 2000 *Gone in 60 Sec-*

onds, which was cited in Disney's annual report as a smash hit. Produced by Jerry Bruckheimer, one of the top producers in Hollywood, and starring Nicholas Cage and Angelina Jolie, the teen car-crash movie cost $103.3 million to make and took in $242 million at the box office. While someone unfamiliar with Mamet's dictum might assume that those holding net points—including the director Dominic Sena, the screenplay writer Scott Rosenberg, and Angelina Jolie—might get a pay-off, here is what happened to the nearly half-billion in revenues it generated at the box office.

Of that $242 million in ticket sales, the theaters kept $139.8 million or nearly 60 percent. So even though Disney's distribution arm, Buena Vista International, is probably Hollywood's most powerful distributor, it got only $102.2 million or about 40 percent of the world box office. From that sum, it deducted $90.6 million for out-of-pocket distribution expenses, which included $67.4 million for buying the ads necessary to reach a global teenage audience, $13 million for prints, and $10.2 million for insurance, shipping, custom fees, check collection, and local taxes, and this left an adjusted gross of just $11.6 million. And from this, the gross players, including Buena Vista (which had a 30 percent distribution fee), Cage, and Bruckheimer, got another $3.4 million. At this point, after the theatrical release, the $103.4 million movie was about $95 million in the red.

THE VIDEO WINDFALL

Six months after the theatrical release, *Gone in 60 Seconds* was released in video stores, and garnered about $198 million in sales. But only a small fraction of this sum, $39.6 million, was credited to the movie because, according to the standard industry contract, it was entitled to only a 20 percent royalty of Buena Vista Home Entertainment's total video and DVD revenues. The $158.4 million balance went to Disney's home entertainment division. From the movie's share of $39.6 million, the distributor deducted $19.7 million for its expenses and fee. The star Nicholas Cage, who had 5 percent of the gross, then got $3.9 million, leaving the movie with only $16 million from the video stores. So even with the video windfall, the movie was still nearly $80 million in the hole.

The net revenue flow came one year later from the pay-TV channels, which paid $18.2 million, which was top dollar because of its box office success. From that Disney deducted $2.7 million to pay the residuals to actors and unions, and

$149,000 for insurance and other expenses. So another $15.4 million was credited to the movie, which would have reduced the movie's deficit to about $63 million, if it were not for the gross players cuts that were added to the deficit and the 10 percent per year interest. As a result of these charges, even with further TV licensing money trickling in, by 2008, *Gone in 60 Seconds* was $155 million in the red. And even with a half-billion gross, the net players would not see a penny.

Disney, which raked in a large percent of the nearly half-billion gross through its ownership of Buena Vista International and Buena Vista Home Entertainment, of course made money, despite the paper losses in its off-the-books entity for *Gone in 60 Seconds*. The net players of course all got paid their fixed compensation. They had willingly agreed to the terms in their contract, which defined their net, and their contracts were almost certainly vetted by their talent agents, business managers, and lawyers, who deal day in and day out with similar contracts. So if the net players are deceived by the contractual definition of net profits, it is, like so many other aspects of Hollywood relationships, a self-deception. They want to believe, no matter what their lawyers, agents, and business managers tell them, that they will participate in the profits of their product.

THE RISE OF DVDS
MPA Studio Revenues from DVD vs.VHS
Studio receipts
(Billions of dollars)

Year	DVD	VHS	Total
1993	0	5.9	5.9
1997	0	9.8	9.8
2002	10.39	5.929	16.3
2003	14.9	3.9906	18.9
2004	18.8	2.1	20.9
2005	20.8	.6	21.4
2006	19.1	.2	19.3
2007*	17.8	.1	17.9

*The studios stopped furnishing these revenue numbers to the MPA in 2008.

NOBODY GETS GROSS

Hollywood studios never give participants—not even ones as powerful as Arnold Schwarzenegger, Tom Cruise, Tom Hanks, Jerry Bruckenheimer, Steven Spielberg, or even Pixar Animation Studios—an unadulterated percentage of the box office gross, or the video store gross, or any other retail gross. As one top Viacom executive explained, "The first truism of Hollywood is: Nobody gets gross—not even a top first dollar gross player."

What the top gross players do get are two kinds of compensation: fixed and contingent. The fixed part is the up-front money that gross players are paid whatever happens to the movie. The contingent part is the percentage of a pool—called the "distributor's adjusted gross" in Hollywood lawyer lingo—that the players get after certain conditions are met, such as the movie earning back the amount of fixed compensation or reaching a contractually-defined cash breakeven point. The pool is "filled" with the money that the distribution arm collects or, in the case of DVDs, gets credited with. With movies, the pool (eventually) gets the remittance from theaters left over after the theater owners deduct their share of ticket-sales and house allowance and after the distributor deducts off the top expenses, such as check collection, currency transfers, stamp taxes, duties, and trade association fees.

To see how these gross participations work in practice, look again at Arnold Schwarzenegger's thirty-three-page contract for *Terminator 3*, which is still considered the gold standard for the super-gross players. For his fixed compensation, Schwarzenegger received $29.25 million—then a record sum. He got the first $3 million on signing and the balance during the course of principal photography. His contingent compensation was 20 percent of the adjusted gross receipts of the distributors (Warner Bros. in the US, Sony Pictures, and Intermedia abroad). The adjusted part of the equation allowed the studio to deduct the items specified on page three of the contract: All industry-standard and customary off-the-top exclusions and deductions, i.e. checking, collection conversion costs, quota costs, trade association fees, residuals, and taxes. Schwarzenegger's lawyer Jacob Bloom is without peer in the entertainment business, but the best he could do here was to cap some of the collection charges at $250,000; he could not touch the residuals or tax deduction. Bloom did manage to get the all-important DVD royalty contribution to the pool raised to 35 percent (although only for Schwarzenegger). As good as this was, it meant that Schwarzenegger was entitled to only 7 percent of what the studios took in from their DVD sales.

Schwarzenegger's contingent compensation would not kick in until the film met the breakeven point defined in the contract. Although the film achieved a $428 million world box office gross, it just barely reached its cash breakeven point, so, alas, Governor Schwarzenegger has earned only a pittance so far from his gross participation beyond his $29.25 million payday. Tom Cruise got a more immediate slice of the action for *Mission Impossible 2*. In return for his producing, acting, guaranteeing against cost overruns, and paying other gross players their share—including Director John Woo's 7.5 percent—Cruise's production company got 30 percent of Paramount's adjusted gross receipts.

In this light, Peter Jackson's compensation for *King Kong* was a relative bargain. Universal paid $20 million in fixed compensation to Jackson's production company not only for his directing services, but also for the script writing and producing services of his collaborators Fran Walsh and Philippa Boyens. And, making a sweet deal even sweeter, the New Zealand citizenship of Jackson and his team qualified Universal for a cash subsidy from the New Zealand government that could be as high as $20 million (and, by itself, that subsidy could pay Jackson's entire fixed compensation). In addition, once the fixed compensation is earned back, Jackson's company also got 20 percent of Universal's adjusted gross receipts, which means it got at least an additional $20 million from movie rentals (which now have passed $200 million worldwide) as well as a huge payoff from future DVDs and television rights.

Such deals are costly, but not crazy. The studios' business nowadays is entirely driven by huge franchises that serve as worldwide licensing platforms. And the most predictable rainmakers for these windfalls, such as Steven Spielberg, George Lucas, Tom Cruise, Jerry Bruckenheimer, and Peter Jackson, are all gross players represented by savvy lawyers and agents who know all the ropes of the movie business. To be sure, not all of their projects turn out to be billion-dollar franchises, but they have little downside. Look at *King Kong*: The upside for Universal was a licensing franchise that would enrich the studio with billions in revenues for years to come. But even if that gamble fails and there are no ape sequels, the studio will lose little, if any money, on the movie itself. In this topsy-turvy world, it makes perfect sense for the studios to recruit the best gross players, as long as the gross they give away is not really the gross.

"I DO MY OWN STUNTS"

Nowhere does Hollywood's culture of deception more clearly manifest itself than on those television talk shows in which stars talk about their movies. The point of this media exercise, at least for the studios releasing the movies, is to fuse the celebrity stars with their fictive movie characters (otherwise the stars might focus interest on themselves instead of the movies being opened). So carefully-designed PR scripts require that the stars "stay in character," as Hollywood calls real life play-acting. When it comes to action movies, the scenario typically calls for stars to tell making-of-movie anecdotes that suggest that they, like the heroes they play on screen, perform death-defying feats. Even if the putative perils are an obvious stretch, they can almost invariably count on a suspension of disbelief on the part of their host-interrogator. Consider, for example, the heroics related on MTV by the three lovely stars of *Charlie's Angels: Full Throttle*, Lucy Liu, Drew Barrymore, and Cameron Diaz. The MTV interviewer, JC Chasez began by asking, "Did you guys do any of your own stunts?"

"We did," Lucy Liu ("Alex") jumps in.

"We get to do all these amazing things," Cameron Diaz ("Natalie") adds, describing by way of example how Drew Barrymore ("Dylan") clung to a speeding car going about "35 miles an hour" while "hitting on the hood of the car"—even after her safety cord came undone. "She's literally hanging on to the car," Liu explains.

At this point in the story, with Barrymore precariously holding onto the hood with one hand

and banging on it with the other, the interviewer asks her excitedly why she didn't yell, "Cut"?

Barrymore ("Dylan") explains despite the danger to herself, she persevered with the shot because "you get so into the adrenaline and you want to be tough.... my character, Dylan, was trying to stop the bad guy." In other words, she had morphed into Dylan—at least in the PR script.

Now back to reality. Stars may have license on talk shows to fantasize about performing perilous stunts such as hanging off the hood of a speeding car, but on a movie set, no matter how willing they may be to risk their lives and limbs, studios will not permit them to take such risks for two reasons.

First, stars often do not have an opportunity to perform stunts because action movies are not shot linearly. The filming is divided between a first unit, "principal photography," that shoots the stars and other actors, and the "second units," which shoot the stunts as well as backgrounds that do not require the presence of the actors. In the James Bond movie *Tomorrow Never Dies*, for instance, this division of labor had five different people playing the James Bond character: Pierce Brosnan, the star, was playing James Bond at the Frogmore Studio outside of London, while four stuntmen at four different locations were playing him in stunts. Similarly, in *Charlie's Angels: Full Throttle*, the "Dylan" character, was played by Drew Barrymore and stuntwomen Heidi Moneymaker, a star gymnast, and Gloria O'Brien. (Lucy Liu's character had four stunt players.)

A second, and even more compelling reason, is the cast insurance requisites. Even if stars are physically present during the shooting of perilous stunts, the production's insurers prohibit them from substituting for the stuntmen. Since Harold Lloyd nearly lost two fingers performing his own stunts in 1920, cast insurance has been an absolute requisite for a Hollywood movie. If a star is deemed an essential element in a movie—as Liu, Diaz, and Barrymore are in *Charlie's Angels: Full Throttle*—and the star becomes disabled, the insurer must cover the resulting loss, which in the case of *Charlie's Angel: Full Throttle* was about $120 million. Before issuing such expensive policies, and no Hollywood movie could be made without one, insurers go to great lengths to make sure that actors do not take any risks that could lead to even a sprained ankle or pulled muscle. Their representatives analyze every shot in the script for potential risks and scrutinize the stars' prior behavior on and off the screen. Once the production starts, they also station hawk-eyed agents on the set to make sure that the stars are not put in harm's way. They might require, for example, that a star standing on a stationary car be held by two safety men (masked in blue spandex so they can be digitally deleted from the final movie). Even if a director or producer were willing to risk injuring a star, the insurer would not allow it. So stars, as much as they might enjoy performing their fantasies, cannot do dangerous stunts for movies.

For the most part, stars do not tell these tall tales of daredevilism on television out of either personal dishonesty, vanity, or egoism. It is their job to play a character in publicity appearances, just as it is the job of studios to hype their movies. Nor do others in these Hollywood productions, even if they were not bound by contractual restrictions on disclosures, or "NDAs," have reason to demystify such off-screen fictionalizing. The subterfuge is part of the system by which studios, talent agencies, music publishers, licensees, and others create, maintain, and profitably exploit the stars' public personalities. The more interesting question: why entertainment journalists, instead of challenging these preposterous claims, act as the stars' smiling attendants on this organized flight from reality? The answer: deception is a cooperative enterprise. By suspending their disbelief, the entertainment journalists get the stars on their programs.

PART III

HOLLYWOOD'S INVISIBLE MONEY MACHINE

WHY *LARA CROFT: TOMB RAIDER* IS CONSIDERED A MASTERPIECE OF STUDIO FINANCING

A Hollywood studio has both an official budget, which is often leaked to trade papers such as *Variety* and *The Hollywood Reporter,* to show how much money it is supposedly costing to produce, and a closely-held production cost budget that shows how much money the movie is actually costing to produce. The latter budget, which is rarely seen by anyone outside of a studio, takes into account the money the studio gets from government subsidies, tax shelter deals, product placement, and other sources that greatly offset the amount of its own money that a studio actually has to sink into a film. A vice president at Paramount explained to me how these invisible maneuvers, including pre-sales abroad, can reduce the risk to practically zero. As an example, he cited Paramount's *Lara Croft: Tomb Raider* as a "minor masterpiece" in the arcane art of studio financing. Although the official budget for this 2001 production was $94 million and reported even higher in the press, the studio's outlay was only $8.7 million. How?

First, Paramount got $65 million from Intermedia Films in Germany in exchange for distribution rights to *Lara Croft: Tomb Raider* for six countries: Britain, France, Germany, Italy, Spain, and Japan. These "pre-sales" left Paramount with the rights to market its film to the rest of the world.

Second, it arranged to have part of the film shot in Britain so that it would qualify for Section 48 tax relief. This allowed it to make a sale-lease-back transaction with the British Lombard Bank through which (on paper only) *Lara Croft: Tomb Raider* was sold to British investors, who collected

a multimillion subsidy from the British government, and then sold it back to Paramount via a
lease and option for less than Paramount paid (in
effect, giving it a share of the tax-relief subsidy).
Through this financial alchemy in Britain, Paramount netted, up front, a cool $12 million. Third,
Paramount sold the copyright through Herbert
Kloiber's Tele Munchen Gruppe, to a German tax
shelter. Because German law did not require the
movie to be shot in Germany, and the copyright
transfer was only a temporary artifice, the money
paid to Paramount in this complex transaction was
truly, as the executive put it, "money-for-nothing."
Through this maneuver, Paramount made another
$10.2 million in Germany, which paid the salaries
of star Angelina Jolie ($7.5 million) and the rest of
the principal cast.

Before the cameras even started rolling, then,
Paramount had earned, risk-free, $87 million. For
arranging this financial legerdemain Paramount
paid about $1.7 million in commissions and fees to
middlemen, but that left it with over $85.3 million
in the bank. So, its total out-of-pocket cost for the
$94-million movie was only $8.7 million.

Since Paramount could be assured of selling
the pay-TV rights to its sister company, Showtime, with which it had an output deal, for $8.5

million, it had little, if any, risk. As it turned out, the movie brought into Paramount's coffers over $100 million from theaters, DVDs, television, and other rights.

Of course, it's not only Paramount that employs these devices. Every studio uses them to minimize risk. In the case of the *Lord of the Rings* trilogy, New Line covered almost the entire cost by using a combination of German tax shelters, New Zealand subsidies, British subsidies, and pre-sales. The lesson here is that things in Hollywood—and especially numbers—are not what they appear to be, proving, yet again, that in Hollywood, the real art of movies is the art of the deal.

MONEY-FOR-NOTHING FROM GERMANY

A loophole in Germany's tax code provided a good portion of the studios' profits at least up until Germany attempted to close it in 2007. This "money for nothing," according to the vice presidents at Paramount responsible for arranging these deals, had been earning annually $70 million to $90 million from them. Best of all, there's no risk or cost for the studio (other than legal fees).

Here's how it works: Germany allows investors in German-owned film ventures to take an immediate tax deduction on their film investments, even if the film they're investing in has not yet gone into production. If a German wants to defer a tax bill to a more convenient time, a good way to do it is by investing in a future movie. The beauty of the German laws as far as Hollywood is concerned is that, unlike the tax laws in other countries, they don't require that films be shot locally or employ local personnel. German law simply requires that the film be produced by a German company that owns its copyright and shares in its future profits. This requisite presents no obstacle for studio lawyers.

The Hollywood studio starts by arranging on paper to sell the film's copyright to a German company. Then, they immediately lease the movie back—with an option to repurchase it later. At this point, a German company appears to own the movie. The Germans then sign a "production service agreement" and a "distribution service agreement" with the studio that limits their responsibility to token and temporary ownership.

For the privilege of fake ownership, the Germans pay the studio about 10 percent more than they'll eventually get back in lease and option payments. For the studio, that extra 10 percent is instant profit. If studio executives don't crow in public about such coups, it's probably out of fear that such publicity will induce governments to stiffen their rules—as, for example, Germany periodically attempts to do by amending its tax code. When you've got a golden goose, you don't want to kill it while it's still laying eggs.

HOW DOES A STUDIO MAKE A WINDFALL OUT OF BEING ON THE LOSING SIDE OF A JAPANESE FORMAT WAR?

Although rarely, if ever, discussed outside a corporate inner sanctum, studios make so-called replication output deals in which studios get paid large amounts from Japanese and other foreign manufacturers to support their formats. Consider, for example, Paramount and Dreamworks' win-win replication deal with Toshiba. In August 2007, in a last desperate effort to prevent its waning HD-DVD format from losing out to Sony's Blu-ray format, Toshiba offered Paramount and Dreamworks (which Paramount distributes) $150 million to put out the high-definition versions of their movies exclusively as HD-DVD. In such deals, the DVD manufacturer pays studios up front cash for the right to make its DVDs. Supposedly, it is an advance that the manufacturer eventually gets back from selling the DVDs back to the studio's video division in much the same way a publisher earns back the advance it gives an author. In this case, Toshiba paid Paramount and Dreamworks a cool $150 million advance even though sales of HD-DVDs were so meager in 2007 that Toshiba was unlikely to ever earn back the entire advance. The wrinkle to the deal was that the studios, Paramount and Dreamworks, agreed not to continue releasing their movies in the rival Blu-ray format.

For Paramount, it was a particularly sweet deal because the payment was booked as a "reduction in cost of goods" for its Home Video division, which meant it did not have to allocate it to any of the titles released on DVD, or share it with writers, directors, stars, other participants, or even equity partners. Then came the real windfall: in March 2008, Toshiba abandoned the HD-DVD format, so the studios got to keep almost all of the $150 million, and then re-released all their movies in the winning Blu-ray format.

Replication output deals go all the way back to the days of videos, when in 1981 Thomas McGrath, a Harvard MBA at Columbia, pioneered them. They rapidly became part of Hollywood's invisible money-making apparatus. Paramount, for example, made a quarter of billion dollars from just three deals: $50 million dollars from Toshiba for agreeing to release *Titanic* on DVD in time for Christmas sales, $150 million from Panasonic for agreeing to allow them take over video replication from another manufacturer (Thompson), and $50 million from the law firm of Ziffrin, Brittenham and Circuit City stores for agreeing to support the DIVX format. Since the DIVX format was never launched, Paramount got to keep the money.

The $150 million Toshiba paid Paramount and Dreamworks not to release their titles on Blu-ray was a worthy continuation of this tradition. Such windfalls, even if not visible to the public, are what assure studios a true Hollywood Ending: bottom-line profits even when their films fail at the box office.

ROMANCING THE HEDGE FUNDS

Ever since Hollywood established its powerful hold over the global imagination, its studios have sought outside investors to help pay for their movies. The list of these "civilians" stretches from William Randolph Hearst, Joe Kennedy, and Howard Hughes in the 1920s to Edgar Bronfman, Sr., Mel Simon, Paul Allen, and Philip Anschutz in more recent times. Some such super-rich investors wanted to participate in the selection, casting, and production of the movies. (Hearst, Kennedy, and Hughes, for example, all insisted that their mistresses be given choice roles.) Other civilians, such as the thousands of investors in Disney's Silver Screen partnerships, sought only the tax-sheltering benefits, but the IRS almost entirely eliminated this loophole by the early 1980s. And some civilians, including hedge funds, actually thought they could make money by negotiating more favorable deals with the studios.

But whatever motives such civilians may have for putting money in Hollywood movies, why do studios want outside funding? When I put the question to a thirty year veteran of studio corporate financing in December 2008, he shot back:

"No journalist who has ever written about movie financing has ever bothered to ask the question: why are the world's largest and most solvent media companies raising outside capital? Journalists all seem buy, hook, line, sinker, and press release, the line that we [studios] need money." He noted that it was in a studio's interest to cry poverty, if only to get stars and their agents to reduce their demands for compensation, adding, "In my thirty years in this business I have never ceased to be amazed by this gullibility." Yes, studios can self-finance their entire slate of movies, and, unlike independent producers, they have sufficient revenues flowing from licensing of DVDs and TV rights to meet any film financing needs. The reason for recruiting outside financing is that the studios can make an "asymmetric deal" with an outsider, which means the outside investor gets a smaller share of the total earnings than does the studio on an equal investment of capital. And it is not only journalists who are gullible. Take JP Morgan Chase, which sent out a "teaser" to hedge funds, reading, "Despite compelling economic returns, major film studios are capital constrained and often must seek co-financing arrangements with other studios and other outside sources," and offered hedge funds "a unique opportunity to participate in the most profitable segment of the motion picture industry."

Hedge funds brimming with excess capital— at least up until the crash in 2008—made perfect civilian recruits for Hollywood, except that hedge fund managers had neither the expertise nor time to evaluate the prospects of individual films. In

2003, Isaac Palmer, then a young senior vice president at Paramount, came up with a brilliant solution. Studios could offer hedge funds a cut of their internal rate of return. This internal rate of return is not limited to so-called "current production," or the theatrical releases, on which studios almost always lose money. Rather, the rate subsumes every penny the studio makes from every source including pay-TV, DVDs, licensing to cable and network television, in-flight entertainment, foreign pre-sales, product placement, and toy licensing. So, even in a bad year, such as 2003, when Paramount released enough bombs to get the studio head fired, its internal rate of return was around 15 percent. This return also included the profits from the company's copyright lease-back sales to foreign tax shelters. (Palmer himself had structured one such deal that netted Paramount $130 million.) Plus, if the studio has a single big breakout movie, as it did in 1999-2000 with *Titanic*, the internal rate of return could leap to as high as 23 to 28 percent.

A safe 15 percent return, with a possible kicker in the event of a hit, proved very attractive to Wall Street. Palmer and his associates at Paramount worked out a deal with Merrill Lynch through which the hedge funds put up 18 percent of the capital for twenty-six consecutive Paramount movies in 2004 and 2005 through a vehicle called Melrose Investors, which then was extended through 2007. What makes this deal asymmetric is that Paramount also took a 10 percent distribution fee off the top on all the revenues, money which the hedge funds do not share. Since this cut comes from the gross, it makes Paramount, but not the hedge fund, a dollar-one gross player in its own movies.

Other studios had even sweeter or more asymmetric deals with hedge funds. Legendary Pictures, for example, was organized as a vehicle through which hedge funds, such as AIG Direct Investments and Bank of America Capital Investors, could sink a half-billion dollars into Warner Bros. movies. But, unlike the Melrose Partners deal, the Legendary Pictures investors do not participate in the entire slate of Warner Bros. movies, which means that they do not really participate in the internal rate of return.

In its asymmetric deals with Wall Street studios enhance their own returns by getting a distribution fee on their investors' share of the revenues. And remain true to the Hollywood tradition of giving civilian investors the short end of the stick.

EVER WONDER WHY THE US LOOKS LIKE CANADA IN THE MOVIES?

In the golden era of the studio system, a studio mainly confined its principal photography to its own highly-efficient sound stages and back lots, where it could deploy its contract stars and technicians, and had whatever exotic material was necessary shot by a traveling second unit. Nowadays, movies are shot all over the world, but in scouting locations, producers are not seeking the most authentic settings or spectacular production values. The lure is government subsidies. As one producer put it, movies, like ladies of the night, go where the money is. Such subsidies can finance up to a large share of the below-the-line budget through a series of maneuvers in which a movie first qualifies for tax credits by employing local actors and technicians, then selling those credits.

Hence the appeal of Canada. The Canadian federal government provides foreign producers with a subsidy, called the Film Production Services Tax Credit, which in 2008 equaled 16 percent of Canadian labor costs. In addition, British Columbia offers an additional 18 percent rebate on labor from that province. Finally, there is a 20 percent break on digital effects, if they are done in Canada.

In order to qualify for this tax credit—which the producer sells through a Canadian partner—either the director or the screenwriter and one of the two highest paid actors must be Canadian, which might partly explain the demand for Canadian actresses, such as Alex Johnson, the star of *Final Destination 3*.

Heeding the siren call of subsidies, Hollywood moved north over the last decade, outsourcing to Canada no fewer than 1,500 movies and television productions. Producers found Vancouver could double for middle America, Toronto could stand in for New York City (especially if the director avoids wide shots), and Calgary makes for a great American West. At times, some script adjustments were required to accommodate the cold reality of the North. For example, in *Final Destination 3*, which was filmed in British Columbia, the climactic attack was supposed to occur during an outdoor party on the Fourth of July but since it was not feasible to have actors wear summery clothes during Vancouver's chilly spring, the holiday was changed to the town's tricentennial celebration. But for Hollywood's illusion-makers, who have much experience in geographically deluding audiences, such adjustments are worthwhile, especially if they finance one third or so of the budget with a depressed currency, the plummeting Canadian loonie. As a result of this location shopping, Canada has emerged as a Hollywood stand-in for America.

PUSHING THE PSEUDO REALITY ENVELOPE

When the *Wall Street Journal* cited the on-screen brand choices of two movie stars, Steve Martin driving a Mercedes Benz S-Class sedan in *Shopgirl* and Matthew Broderick driving one in *The Stepford Wives,* as empirical evidence that this model of Mercedes has practically become an icon for corporate chieftains, movie stars, and diplomats, it showed how effective product placement can be in movies. It was not the movie stars themselves who drive that brand of car, but their fictional characters who are cast with those cars by the producers.

The casting of cars goes back to the 1974 James Bond film *The Man with the Golden Gun*, whose producer, Albert "Cubby" Broccoli, made a deal to use American Motors vehicles in all the chase scenes in exchange for advertising dollars to promote the movie. The function of such product placement is to subtly associate the car brand with a class of people. Hence the choice of Chrysler

Jeeps in *Lara Croft: Tomb Raider 2*, Audis in *I, Robot* and *The Transporter 2*, General Motors cars in *The Matrix Reloaded*, and Ford cars on *X-Files* and *24*. Product placement now includes products ranging from Apple computers in *Mission: Impossible* to Nokia phones in *The Saint* to almost any brand mentioned on NBC's *The Apprentice*.

The persistence of a brand in a studio's movies often signifies nothing more than a package deal. The Weinstein Company, for example, entered into a multi-year marketing alliance with L'Oréal Paris, the world's largest "beauty" brand, which will result in the integration of L'Oréal's products in the Weinstein brothers' movies. And, with digital technology, even if a L'Oréal product was not shot in the movie itself, it can be inserted later (as is now being done with old TV series). One successful producer, whose movies have been distributed by the Weinstein brothers, noted "Product placement gigs will become a major source of production financing in the future, in which a movie provides a controlled world of good-looking stars wearing a certain brand of clothing for an hour and a half, in exchange for which the brand manufacturer pays for a large share of the production."

Product placement, though at a much smaller (and discrete) scale, has a long history in Hollywood. In the 1930s, De Beers, for example, had its agents give studio executives sample diamonds to use in roles that showed women being swayed by the gift of a diamond jewel. Not uncommonly, the diamonds were never returned. As brands took on more global significance, product placement became more open—and routine. Most product placements nowadays are barter deals. A manufacturer finances a cross-promotional ad campaign in return for their product being placed in a movie. In more recent James Bond movies, such as *Die Another Day* and *The World Is Not Enough*, for example, such ads for product placement deals were valued at over $30 million dollars. Cash deals are much rarer—and minuscule by comparison—but can prove useful in covering unforeseen contingencies. In *Terminator 3*, for example, the cash committed for product placements was used to guarantee the deferred part of Jonathan Mostow's $4,960,000 director's fee.

Not all product placement deals accrue to the profit of the production itself. In the case of *Natural Born Killers*, for example, a producer arranged for the director Oliver Stone and other members of the production to get two free pairs of cowboy boots in return for showing the boots' brand name, Abilene, on a truck passing by the open convertible driven by the character Mallory Knox (Juliette Lewis). This meant that the two vehicles—Mallory's car and the

Abilene boot truck—coming from opposite directions, had to arrive in front of the camera at precisely the same time. Over and over again, both drivers, starting their approach a half mile apart, had to be continually cued with walkie-talkies as the camera, which was mounted on a crane, swooped down. So, to get his free boots, Stone had to shoot numerous retakes, which delayed a production running at $300,000 a day.

For smaller independent movies, the fees for product placement, whether cash or barter, are much less. The going rate for a single product inclusion in an independent movie usually ranges between $50,000–250,000. According to one knowledgeable independent producer, the most that's gained from the placements is some free products, some cash for the production, and some shared advertisement placement, and that is usually conditioned on the product making the final cut and the film getting a US release. Even so, for productions on a tight budget, bartering airplane tickets, hotel rooms and automobile leases for product placement slots can result in more money being available for the filming itself—or post-production work. Nor is there any reason that product placement should not be part of the pseudo-reality of a movie. All the Oscar ceremony blather about social reality notwithstanding, movies are fictive concoctions. What goes into that concoction—including stars chosen for their ability to pre-sell foreign markets, locations chosen to qualify for government subsidies, and brands chosen for their production placement value—doesn't alter its fictional status. The only problem comes when the illusion of a movie is confused with the reality of the consumer zeitgeist—which of course is the ultimate purpose of the product placer.

THE NEW CIVIL WAR AMONG THE STATES

Not willing to leave all the glamor of providing backdrops for Hollywood movies to Canadian interlopers, states are now competing against each other to lure studios with lucrative incentives to shoot movies in their bailiwick. The incentive usually takes the form of awarding state tax credits to a movie, which a studio can then sell to corporations or individuals able to use them to offset their taxes. Warner Bros. and Paramount's 2008 film *The Curious Case of Benjamin Button* is a case in point. The film had been budgeted at over $160 million because of expensive computer-generated special effects needed in postproduction to age and de-age the characters played by Brad Pitt and Cate Blanchett. The producers figured out that by filming it in Louisiana—for example, substituting the Gulf coast at Mandeville for the English Channel—they could qualify for the tax credit not only on the scenes actually shot in Louisiana but also for the special effects done in Los Angeles-as-Louisiana. They were also awarded a 15 percent tax credit for the entire budget of the film, including the money spent out of state on special effects and other post production work. As a result, the producers were able to cash in $27,117,737 from these tax credits, a windfall they would have missed had they shot the movie in Hollywood. Of course, this largesse proved costly to Louisiana. In 2006, it doled out $121 million in tax credits and, after it was discovered that producers might be paying counter-bribes to qualify, the Louisianan who oversaw the program, Mark Smith, pleaded guilty to taking $67,500 in bribes to inflate production budgets for film companies. Even so, in 2008, more than seventy films and TV productions qualified for tax credits in Louisiana.

By 2008, no fewer than forty states were offering some kind of incentive to lure movies. Most used the same form of tax credit as Louisiana, which is then "monetized" for the studios by specialized financial companies, such as Screen Capital International. A few states simply rebate a percentage of the budget to the studio. New Mexico, for example, gives a 25 percent production cost rebate. As far as studios are concerned, the more the merrier, and the more complex the better. The incentive war between the states is just another opportunity for enrichment.

THE RISE AND FALL OF PAY TELEVISION

In Hollywood, like its movies, El Dorados are found and lost. Consider the once rich pay-channel output deals, which, as late as July 2008, Bob Weinstein, the co-chairman of the Weinstein Company, could describe as "the bedrock of the business… not one company in this business could survive and succeed without one."

These quasi-secret deals originated back in the early 1980s, when Viacom's Showtime was desperately competing with Time Inc.'s HBO for access to cable viewers. These were known in the industry as "The Pay-TV Wars." In those years, when DVDs were no more than a distant gleam in the eyes of Japanese manufacturers and videos were rented but not sold to the public, studio movies on pay channels drove cable subscriptions, and to get those subscriptions cable operators would pay big money to the dominant pay-TV channel, which was HBO. In this battle to dominate cable distribution, a battle HBO won, the pay channels needed the exclusive rights to movies, and offered to buy studios' entire slate of movies for many years. Although this war was rarely, if ever, mentioned in the entertainment media, many of the executives who negotiated these early deals, including Frank Biondi, Jonathan Dolgen, and Thomas McGrath, went on to run Hollywood studios. The price that was paid per title was adjusted by a formula that adjusted the payout, which averaged about $12 million, according to its box office results. In 1985, however, after HBO wound up paying $30 million for *Ghostbusters* because of its huge box office numbers, it began capping the maximum pay out at $12.5 million per title. So did the other pay-TV channels. Even so, payment to studios averaged close to $10 million a title up until 2005. A studio with twenty-five movies a year in its output deal would collect a quarter billion dollars in the US alone. This was pure gold since, unlike the theatrical release, in which theaters keep half of the box office, and then distributors deduct print and advertising outlay from what remains, almost all the money from the output deal went directly into the studios' coffers. And by 2000, the six major studios, and their subsidiaries, were taking in $1.1 billion from pay-TV.

In the new millennium, however, the ascendancy of the DVD in the 2000s, and later iTunes and other digital downloads, gave viewers alternative ways of watching movies in high quality at home before they became available on cable. In addition, according to a top executive of HBO, new subscription growth was flattening, movies or no movies, with the near saturation of household growth. To hold their audience, and cash in on the DVD boom, pay channels increased their investment in original programming, such as the series *Sex and the City*, *The Sopranos*, and *The L Word*. As a result, as the studios' multi-year output deals expired, the pay-TV channels drove harder and harder bargains with studios, and became far more selective about what they would buy. Instead of buying a studio's entire output, pay channels found they could fill a large part of their 24-hour a day schedule by simply replaying more frequently their own inventory of movies and original programs. By 2009, they were buying less than half the number of studio movies that they had bought in 2005, and paying half the price per title.

One of the first casualties of this cutback was New Line Cinema, a mini-studio that Time Warner had acquired in 1996. Up until 2007, it had an output deal with HBO, another Time Warner subsidiary, that guaranteed it about $80 million for twelve movies. When Jeff Bewkes became chairman of Time Warner in 2008, he found that HBO did not need the New Line movies, and the $80 million was largely being used to finance distribution organizations that could be folded into Warner Brothers. So Bewkes ended the sweetheart output deal, closed New Line (as well as its Fine Line and Picturehouse divisions) and did not renew the contracts of New Line co-founders Bob Shaye and Michael Lynne.

Paramount had a similar problem in 2008 with its output deal with Showtime after the pay channel became part of CBS, Inc. in the split up of Viacom. Unwilling to renew the rich sweetheart contract it signed with Paramount when both companies were part of Viacom, Showtime left Paramount without any output deal.

But don't cry yet for Hollywood. Even though the gold is gradually petering out of the pay-TV

El Dorado, it is because new ones are emerging on the digital horizon.

FOR WHOM DOES THE MOVIE BUSINESS TOLL?

Along the metaphoric road to getting movies to the greater public, the studios act as the toll collector. The major studios collect this toll in the form of a distribution fee not only on the movies that they produce and finance but on other people's movies that they distribute. No matter how well or badly a movie fares at the box office, no matter how much money outside investors have sunk into it, the studio takes its cut from the gross emanating from the box office, the video store, and the television stations. Each of the six big studios, Warner Bros., Disney, Fox, Sony, Paramount, and Universal, has a wholly owned distribution arm that distributes titles that it finances, titles that it co-finances with partners, and titles produced and financed by outside production companies and so-called studio-less studios. The reason that these six studios dominate distribution is that the multiplex owners who book movies believe that they alone have the wherewithal not only to open a movie in 3,000 or more theaters on any given weekend but to create a national audience for it.

The studios are in this powerful position because they have accrued over the past three decades an enormous reservoir of intangible good will with the chains that own the multiplexes by granting them such favors as readjusting the terms of their poorly-performing movies, extending their payment period, carving out zones to avoid destructive competition between the multiplexes, and providing them with a constant diet of franchised movies, such as *Pirates of the Caribbean, Spider-Man,* and *Harry Potter,* that fill their theaters with popcorn consumers. In return, the chains have given these studios a large measure of effective control over the booking and staging of wide openings, for example, inserting teaser trailers months in advance of the opening so that they can more precisely coordinate the marketing campaign. So if outside producers and financiers want to play in this game of wide-opening movies, which is where the big grosses are found, they have little choice but to pay the studios' price of admission: the distribution fee.

The fee varies according to the strength of the players. Studios usually charge a 30 percent distribution fee on the films they themselves finance. In Hollywood accounting, each of its movies is set up as an independent off-the-books company, and the 30 percent fee is treated as a cost paid to an outside entity, even though the distributor is also fully owned by the same studio. The result of this fictional division is that a film, after paying this enormous tariff, rarely shows a profit, even if the studio is making a profit from the distribution fee, and so the writers, directors, actors, and other participants in the profit rarely see anything but red ink on their semi-annual statements.

When it comes to films that are financed by other people's money, the distribution fee is the subject of often contentious negotiations. Most outsiders needing to reach a wide audience wind up paying about 18 percent. Since the actual cost of distributing a movie is 8 percent, a figure which includes the incremental cost of PR specialists, media buyers, customs clearance, transportation, and lawyers' time, the studio makes as pure profit 10 percent of the gross revenues of a film on which some other party financed and took all the risk. Stronger players often negotiate the fee down to 12 percent, but that still leaves the studio a 4 percent profit on their gross, and hedge funds, which co-invest in entire slates of studio films, pay only 10 percent, yielding still a 2 percent profit. There are also "a few gorillas," as a Paramount exec calls them, whose movies are so vital to studios, that they pay only 8 percent, the magic number at which the studio makes no profit.

But such nonprofit arrangements are the exception, numbering in 2008, according to the Paramount executive, only three: Steven Spielberg's deal with Universal, and Dreamworks Animation and Marvel Entertainment's deals with Paramount. Most of these studio distribution deals with outsiders yield substantial profits on Other People's Money. A top executive at Disney calculated, for example, that Disney made over $80 million in 2005 from outsiders (after deducting its actual costs of distribution). This skim, which goes to the bottom line, makes the six studios the biggest gross players in Hollywood.

PART IV

HOLLYWOOD POLITICS

IN THE PICTURE

In November 2009, Oliver Stone literally put me in the picture. I was seated at an oval table under an eerie light in what purported to be the office of the Chairman of New York Federal Reserve Bank. As the meeting continued throughout the night, people around screamed about the 'moral hazard' of saving a failing investment bank. At one point, there was even a call from the White House dooming the bank in question. The frenetic scene is no more than a consensual hallucination directed by Oliver Stone for the movie *Wall Street 2: Money Never Sleeps*. (A sequel to his 1987 *Wall Street*.) The magnificently wood-paneled room is actually the executive conference room of an insurance company, MetLife, which is serving as a location for this part of the filming. The eerie glow comes from powerful lamps ingeniously suspended from helium balloons above us. The shouting is coming from actors Frank Langella, Eli Wallach, and Josh Brolin. Although I had only a bit part in this drama, it provided me with an opportunity to see how a Hollywood movie is made from the vantage point of the set.

The project was initiated in 2005 by Edward R. Pressman, the producer of the original *Wall Street*, after he saw the fictional villain of *Wall Street* Gordon Gekko (portrayed by Michael Douglas) on the cover of *Fortune*, accompanied by a headline about the return of greed to Wall Street. Pressman reasoned that if eighteen years after the movie, Gekko was still the media's icon for greed on Wall Street, a sequel was in order. He owned the rights for the sequel but sought to interest Twentieth Century Fox, which had distributed the original *Wall Street*. Getting a movie made in Hollywood when the hero is not a comic book character was not an easy task. Just getting a script that was acceptable to Fox took four years—and three different (and very expensive) writers. Even then Fox's approval was conditional on the stars and director, as are almost all movie deals. Pressman persuaded Michael Douglas to again play Gekko, a role for which he had won the Oscar in 1988, and Oliver Stone (who had dropped out of the project earlier), to direct. Fox then agreed to finance it. Part of the $67 million budget could be retrieved from New York State and New York City's tax credit programs (which effectively reimburse 35 percent of the production budget spent in New York).

The Federal Reserve scenes were filmed over a long weekend about midway in the eleven-week shooting schedule. Through the seemingly endless retakes in which actors repeat virtually the same lines while extras behind them—each of whom is called by a number rather than a name—move to the exact same 'mark,' or position, Stone gradually perfects the illusion. Between each take, the time on the grandfather clock in the office is reset to the exact time as it was at the start of the previous scene. The process is not unlike the never-ending day in *Groundhog Day*. But surrounding the illusion-in-the-making is an envelope of reality. It is peopled by a small army of technicians, including make-up artists, hair stylists, script supervisors, technical advisors, continuity girls, stand-by carpenters, wranglers, costumers, sound boom men, camera operators, film loaders, set decorators, and electricians. They work ceaselessly, rushing onto the set between takes, to maintain and repair the illusion. One of the advantages of a top director such as Stone is that he can get the best of the below-the-line talent, in this case such Oscar nominees as Rodrigo Prieto, the Mexican-born director of photography, whose credits include *Frida, Brokeback Mountain*, and *Babel*; Kristi Zea, the production designer, whose credits include *Revolutionary Road, Goodfellas,* and *The Silence of The Lamb*; and Tod Maitland, the versatile sound technician who won an Oscar for *Seabiscuit*.

Stone himself is constantly moving around the set, viewing scenes from different angles and talking to the actors and extras, often in whispers. At other times, he confers with technical advisors, including two former SEC lawyers who had actually attended the Fed meetings, asking them about such details as how coffee cups would be placed on the table or how precisely a phone call from the White House would be answered. When any unexpected difficulties arise, such as when the camera dolly creaks audibly on its tracks, he jokes with the cast, having a gift for putting actors at ease. But even with the amicable atmosphere, he has to keep the movie running on a tight schedule. Just the below-the-line expenditures for *Wall Street 2*, which does not include the compensation for the stars, writers, producers, or the director, is running about $220,000 a day for interior scenes (exterior and crowd scenes can be much more expensive). So unless he shoots the planned number of script pages a day, he will run over budget. While Hollywood players are often depicted in the media as profligate spenders, the opposite is true when it comes to studio executives supervising a movie that they are financing. Before *Wall Street 2* went into production, Fox went through the budget line by line, squeezing every penny it could out of the budget, even attempting to reduce the fees of major actors (all of whom have a "quote,"or established price per movie.) If the shooting ran over budget, Fox could ask that scenes be cut out of the script to get it back on track or use money from the post-production budget, which includes putting in visual effects (which are crucial in *Wall Street 2* since some scenes are shot with blank backgrounds), adding sound, and editing. So Stone manages to adhere to the schedule, even when it requires him—and his assistant directors—working grueling fourteen hour days (as in the Federal Reserve Bank scenes). And, as it turns out, he completes the movie within a day of the targeted end of shooting.

When I arrive at the wrap party at the club Spin, the cast, crew, and friends are huddled around plasma TV screens, watching clips from the movie. For most of them, it is their first opportunity to see how Stone actually realized the scenes they had worked in or on. As they watch, visibly impressed, they often cheer with the sort of gusto one might expect at a Super Bowl party when a touchdown is scored. Everyone embraces Stone, the hero of the evening, as he passes through the room. The club is owned by Susan Sarandon (who had acted in the movie) and features ping pong tables where Josh Brolin and Mel Gibson (who was not in the movie) engaged in a wild game. The celebration continued into the early hours of the morning.

Unlike independent movies, which usually take years to reach the theaters, studio movies have a built-in release date from the moment they are green-lighted. *Wall Street 2* is scheduled to open at multiplexes across America on April 23, 2010. And during production Fox was already working on the advertising and marketing campaign, which will require a huge investment in ads on cable and network TV in mid-April. The worldwide P&A budget will probably exceed $40 million, which will bring Fox's total outlay to about $100 million. The original *Wall Street* did far better in earning critical acclaim and buzz than money. Fox's share of the American box office was only $20.2 million—and it fared far worse in foreign markets. The problem Fox had then, and faces again, is that movies that involve complex issues, such as a financial crisis on Wall Street, did not draw the teen-age audience conditioned to expect the fast tempo of the studio's superheroes. The $100 million gamble for Fox is that in the pre-summer period, when the herds of teens are still in school, it will be able to find an adult audience for the multiplexes.

PARANOIA FOR FUN AND PROFIT: THE SAGA OF *FAHRENHEIT 9/11*

Michael Moore had a problem in April 2004. He'd finished making *Fahrenheit 9/11* but had no American distributor. Mel Gibson's Icon Productions rejected the project back in April 2003. (Moore claims he had a signed contract before Gibson acquiesced to White House pressure. Icon executives deny any such contract existed.) Moore then went to Harvey Weinstein at Miramax, which since 1993 had been a wholly owned Disney subsidiary. Weinstein agreed to back the movie and signed a contract with Moore to acquire the rights. But in order to distribute the movie, Weinstein still needed the approval of his superiors at Disney because Weinstein's contract explicitly prohibited Miramax, a wholly owned subsidiary of Disney, from distributing any film that was vetoed by the Disney CEO. When then-CEO Michael Eisner exercised his veto in May 2003, Miramax, though it still held the rights to the film, could not distribute *Fahrenheit 9/11*.

By the time Eisner told Weinstein of his decision, the Miramax head had already given Moore $6 million from Miramax's loan account. Weinstein agreed that this advance was to be "bridge financing" that he would recover when he sold off the film's distribution rights. To make sure there was no misunderstanding, Disney's senior executive vice president Peter Murphy, who was also at the meeting, wrote Weinstein a letter on May 12, 2003, affirming that this money was "bridge financing" and that Weinstein had agreed to dispose of Miramax's interest in the film. For Moore, this $6 million in "bridge financing" was more than enough to make *Fahrenheit 9/11*. He acquired most of the footage from television film libraries at little, if any, cost and did not pay any of the on-camera talent (except for himself). On April 13, 2004, after Weinstein saw a rough cut, he went back to Eisner and asked him to reconsider his year-old decision not to distribute *Fahrenheit 9/11*. After getting a report on the content, which included footage from such sources as Al Jazeera and Al-Arabiya television, Eisner saw no reason to change his position. He again declared that Disney wouldn't have anything to do with the movie.

With the presidential election heating up, Moore needed to get his movie into theaters. Although Weinstein had told Eisner and Murphy that he planned to sell the film's distribution rights after it was screened at the Cannes Film Festival, Moore had a more expedient stratagem. On the *Fahrenheit 9/11* DVD, Moore says he resolved to get the film seen in America "by hook or by crook." His hook was censorship.

On May 5, 2004, the *New York Times* ran a front-page article headlined "Disney Is Blocking Distribution of Film That Criticizes Bush." The story included the sensational charge that Eisner "expressed particular concern that [choosing to distribute *Fahrenheit 9/11*] would endanger tax breaks Disney receives for its theme park, hotels, and other ventures in Florida, where Mr. Bush's brother, Jeb, is governor." The source for this allegation was Moore's agent, Ari Emanuel. Two days later, Moore claimed on his Web site that Disney's board of directors rejected *Fahrenheit 9/11* "last week." In fact, the Disney board had not made such a decision in 2004; the project had been vetoed in 2003.

Moore's excursion from reality proved a boon at Cannes. On May 22, 2004, the Cannes jury defied putative efforts to censor Moore by awarding *Fahrenheit 9/11* the prestigious Palme d'Or. Moore now had a golden palm in his hand and the media at his feet. With more free publicity than any Hollywood studio could afford to buy, *Fahrenheit 9/11* now stood to rake in a fortune. And Disney, which still controlled the movie's rights through its subsidiary Miramax, now got to decide who was going to profit from it. Disney had some experience dealing with Miramax's hot potatoes. Rather than distributing the controversial *Kids* and *Dogma*, Disney allowed Miramax founders Harvey and Bob Weinstein to buy the films back and set up short-lived companies to distribute them. But those potatoes were as small as they were hot. In the case of *Fahrenheit 9/11*, Eisner wasn't about to let the windfall escape into the Weinstein brothers' pockets. Nor could Disney take the PR hit that would result from backtracking and distributing the movie itself.

Eisner's solution: Generate the illusion of outside distribution while orchestrating a deal that allowed Disney to reap most of the profits. Here's how the dazzling deal worked. On paper, the Weinstein brothers bought the rights to *Fahrenheit 9/11* from Miramax. The Weinsteins then transferred the rights to a Disney corporate front called Fellowship Adventure Group. In turn, that company outsourced the documentary's theatrical distribution rights (principally to Lions Gate Films, IFC Films, and Alliance Atlantis Vivafilms) and video distribution rights (to Columbia Tristar Home Entertainment).

Because of the buzz now attached to *Fahrenheit 9/11*, Harvey Weinstein extracted extremely favorable terms from these distributors, about one-third of what distributors typically charge. Their cut amounted to slightly more than 12 percent of the total they collected from the theaters. As a result, *Fahrenheit 9/11*'s net receipts, what remains after the distributors deduct their percentage and their out-of-pocket expenses (mounting an ad campaign, making prints, dubbing the film), would be much higher than those of a typical Hollywood film.

Fahrenheit 9/11, now an event, took in more than $228 million in ticket sales worldwide, a record for a documentary, and sold 3 million DVDs, which brought in another $30 million in royalties. After the theaters took their share of the movie's gross (roughly 50 percent) and distributors deducted the marketing expenses (including prints, advertising, dubbing, and custom clearance) and took their own cut, the net receipts returned to Disney were $78 million.

Disney now had to pay Michael Moore's profit participation. Under normal circumstances, documentaries rarely, if ever, make profits (especially if distributors charge the usual 33 percent fee). So, when Miramax made the deal for *Fahrenheit 9/11*, it allowed Moore a generous profit participation—which turned out to be 27 percent of the film's net receipts. Disney, in honoring this deal, paid Moore a stunning $21 million. Moore never disclosed the amount of his profit participation. When asked about it, the proletarian Moore joked to reporters on a conference call, "I don't read the contracts."

What of Disney? After repaying itself $11 million for acquisition costs, it booked a $46 million net profit, which Eisner split between two subsidiaries, the Disney Foundation and Miramax. With his $21 million, Michael Moore had perhaps the happiest ending of all.

THE SAGA CONTINUES

While Disney made a profit on the paranoia in *Fahrenheit 9/11*, it led Eisner and other Disney executives to question whether Harvey Weinstein was worth the trouble he had caused the corporation. While Weinstein told journalists how much money he had made for Disney, an internal audit showed that Miramax under Weinstein, rather than adding to Disney's profits, actually was hemorrhaging rivers of red ink. This reversal of fortune proceeded from a loophole in the original deal that Jeffrey Katzenberg, then Disney's studio head, negotiated with Weinstein in 1993. The Weinsteins had demonstrated a superb gift for finding, shaping, and marketing independent films like *Sex, Lies, and Videotape* and *The Crying Game*. To give the brothers a powerful incentive to ferret out similar arty winners, Disney agreed to give them a performance bonus of between 30 percent and 35 percent of their film profits, a bonus that would be calculated each fiscal year. The deal also tied Miramax's capital budget for acquiring and producing films to its annual performance. So, the more money Miramax made in a fiscal year, the more money the Weinsteins made and the bigger the capital budget of their Miramax division. The loophole was that

Disney agreed to calculate Miramax's profits in a fiscal year solely on the films released that year. In making what seemed like a minor concession to Weinstein so that he could use his discretion in timing the marketing of art films, Disney did not foresee how brilliantly he would game the calendar to create the illusion of profits for Miramax and the reality of huge bonus payments for himself and his brother, Bob. He simply shifted potential money-losing films into future fiscal years so that they didn't reduce either his bonus or Miramax's capital budget. To prevent Weinstein from over-spending, Eisner later imposed a further condition on the deal: For every dollar Miramax exceeded its capital budget, a similar amount was deducted from the Weinsteins' annual bonus. To avoid this penalty, Weinstein could delay releasing high-budget films in years in which he was close to exceeding his capital budget. As a result, even more films got dumped into Weinstein's limbo of unreleased movies. For example, Zhang Yimou's *Hero*, which had been acquired at Sundance in 2002, was held for more than two years so that its nearly $20 million cost would not count against the Weinsteins' bonus. *Hero* was released in 2004, a year less profitable for Miramax in which no bonus would be paid anyway.

In 2005, Eisner decided not to renew the Weinsteins' contract. Whereas Miramax belonged lock, stock, and barrel to Disney, the Weinstein brothers had a claim to subsidiary Dimension Films, which Eisner wanted to keep at Disney. So he had to negotiate an exit package for the Weinsteins. Enter Hollywood lawyer (and Shakespearean scholar) Bertram Fields, who got them a $130 million settlement (partially based on what turned out to be Miramax's phantom profits in prior fiscal years), and allowing Harvey and Bob Weinstein to create a new film company, Weinstein Brothers Pictures.

After their departure, Disney released many of the delayed movies, which produced losses in 2005 alone of over $100 million. Harvey Weinstein, known for his artful films, also demonstrated with Disney that he had mastered the artful deal that amazed even Hollywood.

PLUS ÇA CHANGE: PARAMOUNT'S REGIME CHANGE

The principal asset of a modern studio nowadays, aside from its library of movie titles and other intellectual properties, is its human capital, which includes executives with the negotiating skills, judgment, charm, and goodwill within the industry to get top stars, make favorable production deals, and profitably organize the release of movies. In the spring of 2004, following a string of six box office flop in 2003, Sumner Redstone, the chairman of Paramount's parent company, decided Paramount needed a new infusion of human capital. In the regime change, Jonathan Dolgen and Sherry Lansing, who had run the studio for the past decade, were out. Brad Grey, a dynamic forty-seven-year old television producer and talent manager, would replace them. Even though he had no previous experience in running a movie studio, Redstone gave him a mandate to turn the studio around.

But turn around from what? Despite its flops, the Dolgen-Lansing decade was hardly a disastrous one. During that period, 1994-2004, Paramount released six out of its ten highest grossing films in history, including *Titanic*, the all-time biggest money-maker, and in eight out of their ten years their division (which included television as well movies) scored record profits. They set up lucrative co-production deals with Dreamworks SKG, established the *Mission Impossible* franchise with Tom Cruise, and created three profitable distribution labels—MTV Films, Nickelodeon Films, and Paramount Classics. Dolgen's skill was the art of the deal which reduced Paramount's risk by using Other People's Money, his specialty being off-balance sheet financing and foreign subsidies to pay for a large part of a film's production costs. Through them, Dolgen and Lansing managed to achieve an average return on invested capital of nearly 60 percent during their ten years. Even in their worst year, 2003, they hit their targeted profit numbers.

Enter Brad Grey. He wasted little time in dismantling the team that his predecessors had built. Within six months, almost every senior executive "ankled," as *Variety* colorfully describes exiting a studio, including Rob Friedman, the head of worldwide distribution and marketing; Thomas Lesinski, the president of the Home Video division; Donald DeLine, the head of film production; Jack Waterman, the president of pay-TV; Gary Marenzi, the head of international TV; and Tom McGrath, the architect of the studio's off-balance sheet financing strategy. In all, over 100 executives were either fired or left Paramount in the regime change. "Even by the harsh standards of Hollywood such wholesale bloodletting is unprecedented," one former Paramount executive said in an email.

Gray also cancelled most, if not all, of the movie projects in process in 2005. Letting it be known that Paramount would place less emphasis, as part of the regime change, on deal-driven movies, he cancelled five such projects based on German and Spanish tax deals, which would have produced about $50 million in bottom line profits. (The financial vice president working on these deals, getting the message, promptly resigned.) But replacing such projects, and packaging scripts with stars, directors, and financing, takes many months, if not years. And by the fall of 2005, Paramount still did not have enough viable projects in the pipeline to provide the studio's distribution arm with product for 2006 and 2007. The solution Grey found was for Redstone to buy Dreamworks SKG for $1.6 billion.

To finance this deal, Redstone sold Dreamworks' movie library to hedge funds for $900 million. As a result, Paramount got thirty-odd Dreamworks projects—including *Dreamgirls* and *Transformers*—to replace the Dolgen-Lansing development projects.

The new regime, at Redstone's prodding, also ended its deal with Cruise-Wagner Productions, which had produced not only its *Mission: Impossible* franchise but its other tentpole film, *War of the Worlds*. The decision to end Cruise's contract, despite Redstone's PR jibes at Cruise, was, to quote *The Godfather*, "Not personal, Sonny; it's strictly business." The real problem was the rich split Cruise had negotiated with Paramount—22 percent of the gross revenues received by the studio on the theatrical release and the television licensing and a 12 percent cut of Paramount's total DVD receipts.

While Paramount was busy subsuming (and becoming) Dreamworks, the human capital at Dreamworks, including Steven Spielberg and his creative team, exited Paramount to create a new studio, backed by $500 million in Indian financing, which would be the new Dreamworks—or at least the sequel. Plus Ça Change or, as they say in Hollywood, that's show business.

TOM CRUISE, INC.

The gawkerization of Hollywood, entertaining as it may be to the public, blots out much of the reality underlying the movie business. Witness, for example, the treatment of Tom Cruise after *People* asked on its Web site in May 2005, if his relationship with the actress Katie Holmes represented "1. TRUE ROMANCE" or "2. PUBLICITY STUNT." In this pseudo-poll, in which subscribers with AOL's instant messaging can "vote" as many times as they like (paying a charge each vote), 62 percent of an unknown number of respondents chose "publicity stunt."

Once this statistically meaningless result was sent out on the PR wire, it spawned a frenzy of stories dangling the bizarre idea that the romance had been faked to publicize, in Cruise's case, Paramount's *War of the Worlds* and, in Holmes' case, Warner Bros.' *Batman Begins*. Frank Rich proclaimed in the *New York Times* that the affair was nothing more than "a lavishly produced freak show, designed to play out in real time," and that "the Cruise-Holmes romance is proving less credible to Americans in 2005 than a Martian invasion did to those of 1938." As it turned out, Cruise and Holmes were subsequently engaged, married, and had a child.

What is entirely lost in the fog of media gossip, however, is the entrepreneurial role that Tom Cruise has carved out for himself in the New Hollywood. Consider, for example, the *Mission: Impossible* franchise. When Paramount decided to reinvent its TV series *Mission: Impossible* as a movie, Cruise not only starred in it, but he (along with producer partner Paula Wagner) produced it. In return for deferring his salary, he negotiated a deal for himself almost without parallel in Hollywood. To begin with, he got 22 percent of the gross revenues received by the studio on the theatrical release and the television licensing. The more radical part of the deal involved the video earnings (the deal was negotiated before DVDs replaced video tapes). When videotapes became a cash cow for Hollywood in the 1970s, each studio employed a royalty system in which one of its divisions, the home-entertainment arm, would collect the total receipts from them and pay another one of its divisions, the movie studio, a 20 percent royalty. This royalty became the "gross" number that the studios reported to their partners and participants. The justification for this system was that, unlike other rights, such as television licenses, which require virtually no sales expenses, videos have to be manufactured, packaged, warehoused, distributed, and marketed. So, the home-entertainment arm keeps 80 percent of the proceeds to pay these costs. The stars, directors, writers, investors, actors, guilds, pension funds, and other gross participants get their share of just the 20 percent royalty. If a star were entitled to 10 percent of the video gross, he or she would get 10 percent of the royalty, which, under this system, is only 2 percent of the real gross.

But not Cruise. He insisted on—and received—"100 percent accounting," which means that the studio, after deducting the out-of-pocket manufacturing and distribution expenses, paid Cruise his 22 percent share of the total receipts. As a result, Cruise earned more than $70 million on *Mission: Impossible*, and he opened the door for stars to become full partners with the studio in the so-called back end.

By 2000, the profits from DVDs had begun to alter Hollywood's profit landscape, and since it was now too complicated to track all the expenses, Cruise revised the deal with Paramount for the sequel *Mission: Impossible 2*. His cut of the gross was increased to 30 percent, and, for purposes of calculating his share of the DVDs, the royalty was doubled to 40 percent. So, he would get 12 percent of the total video/DVD receipts with no expenses deducted by Paramount. In return for this amazing deal, Cruise agreed to pay the only other gross participant, the director John Woo, out of his share.

As with *Mission: Impossible*, Cruise's company produced the film, and Cruise, who proved to be a relentlessly focused producer, brought *Mission: Impossible 2* in on budget. The movie went on to be an even bigger success than the original, earning more than a half-billion dollars at the box office and selling over 20 million DVDs. Cruise's share amounted to $92 million—and he was now the key element in Paramount's most profitable franchise. In light of such a success, Paramount initially agreed on the same deal with Cruise for *Mission: Impossible 3*. Even with Cruise's rich cut, Paramount would make money. According to an internal analysis by Paramount, each DVD, which retails for about $15 wholesale, costs the company only $4.10 to manufacture, distribute, and market. Another 45 cents goes for residuals payments to the guilds, unions, and pension plans, leaving the studio with slightly over $10. So, even after giving Cruise his cut of $1.80 per DVD, Paramount stood to make more than $8 per DVD.

By 2004, DVDs were bringing into the studios' coffers more than twice as much money as the theatrical release of movies, and there was every reason to assume that *Mission: Impossible 3* would sell more DVDs than its predecessor. The budget, however, had increased to $180 million, so new Paramount studio chief, Brad Grey, asked for a renegotiation. After the dust had cleared, Cruise still had his huge percentage of the gross—it actually had improved since there were now no other gross participants. When released in 2006, the movie took in $397.8 million at the box office (nearly 70 percent of which came from foreign theaters)—

which was less than the prior sequel—but Cruise's real profit came in his huge 12 percent cut of DVD sales. As it turned out, Cruise was now making much more from the franchise than Paramount, a disparity that so infuriated Paramount owner Sumner Redstone that he terminated Cruise's contract with Paramount in August 2006.

But Cruise did not go unemployed. MGM hired him in November 2006 to revive United Artists, a studio originally created in 1916 by such legendary Hollywood stars as Charlie Chaplin, Mary Pickford, and Douglas Fairbanks, Jr. but which had been dormant for twenty years. Merrill Lynch organized a $500 million line of credit to finance this enterprise. Whether or not Cruise can relaunch a moribund studio remains to be seen, but Cruise, as one of the handful of producers—along with George Lucas, Steven Spielberg, and Jerry Bruckheimer—who can reliably deliver a billion-dollar franchise, may yet succeed.

AN EXPERT WITNESS IN WONDERLAND

In 2005, I became an expert witness in a Hollywood lawsuit that in nearly five years managed to consume over $20 million in legal fees. (And, as of 2010, an appeal is sill pending.) The heart of this Dickensian litigation was a contract between an author and producer for the making of *Sahara*, a $130 million action movie released in 2005 that starred Penelope Cruz and Matthew McConaughey, and was directed by Breck Eisner (the son of ex-Disney chairman Michael Eisner). The plaintiff was the author Clive Cussler, who had sold the film rights to his 1992 bestselling book *Sahara* for $10 million, and charged in his suit that his right to approve the final script had not been honored. He was represented in this suit by Hollywood lawyer Bertram Fields, who, according to his legend, had never lost a case (which is less impressive than it sounds because most Hollywood cases are settled out of court and the results are sealed). The defendant was Crusader Entertainment, a production company owned by oil tycoon Philip Anschutz, who, aside from his media properties, owned the majority stake in Regal Entertainment, America's largest movie theater chain. Anschutz, who was listed by *Forbes* as the thirty-sixth richest man in America with $8 billion in assets, was represented by O'Melveny & Myers, a legal powerhouse, which according to *American Lawyer*, had the top-rated litigation department in the country.

The two law firms were located almost directly across the street from one another on the Avenue of the Stars in Century City, which once was the back lot of 20th Century Fox.

O'Melveny & Myers star litigator Alan Rader, who co-managed the *Sahara* case, retained me as an expert witness in 2005. He said that he had read my writings on the logic of Hollywood and wanted me to objectively lay out for the jury, possibly in a PowerPoint presentation, the economic reality behind the movie business. To prepare, I had to review a vast array of contracts, distribution deals, financial analyses, and other paperwork that might help me explain the requisites of the movie business. I also had to provide a lengthy deposition in Bert Fields' offices. Then, after years of convoluted maneuvering, the case actually went to trial, a rarity in Hollywood law. Six weeks later, the jury provided a surprise ending to the drama: Bert Fields, the man who putatively never lost a case, lost big for his client. Clive Cussler was ordered not only to pay Anschutz's company $5 million for undermining the success of the movie, but he had to pay him a staggering $13.9 million to cover his legal costs. In addition to this $18.9 million, Cussler also had to pay his own legal bill to Bert Fields, which presumably was also sizable.

Leaving aside the brilliant lawyering on both sides, the material I reviewed provided me with a key insight into how Hollywood works: the movie-business is a fee-driven business. When viewed from the outside, movies, which are almost always set up as separate off-the-books entities, rarely, if ever, show a profit. Nevertheless, when viewed from the inside, they serve as vessels for collecting and dispensing billions of dollars in fees. In 2008, the fees from studio movies alone exceeded $8 billion. And these fees support a large part of the Hollywood community, including directors, stars, producers, and screenwriters, as well as the talent agents, business managers, and lawyers who represent them. But most of these fees are paid only if the production is approved, or green-lit, by a studio willing to finance it. So the big players in Hollywood, and their representatives, have a powerful incentive to use whatever means at their disposal to pressure studio executives into green-lighting their projects. For their part, studios also get a rich fee, a distribution fee, which allows then to take a percentage off the top from every dollar that comes from every source including theaters, in-flight entertainment, DVDs, and television licensing. This percentage can be as high as 33 percent or as low as 10 percent depending on the relative negotiating strength of each party. Before giving the green-light, studios run the numbers to make sure that their distribution fee has a good chance of covering their outlay, even if the film itself is unprofitable for others. Once a studio provides a green-light, the studio deposits money in its account, and the production can pay all the fees and salaries necessary to make the movie.

How do studios get the money to finance this fee-driven economy? To begin with, they raise a substantial part this sum by wheeling and dealing with outside parties. This includes negotiating tax credit deals around the world with financial groups needing tax relief, lease-back deals on copyright of the titles, pre-sales agreements to sell rights to foreign markers, product placement deals with corporations to insert their product or brands in their films, and hedge fund investments. This deal-making employs a large part of the entertainment law establishment who churn out the necessary paperwork. It also often provides, depending on the film, between 20 and 60 percent of the budget. For the balance of the money, studios either use their cash flow from previous films or borrow from banks through their revolving lines of credit at banks, called "revolvers," assuming, based on their financial analysis, that they will earn back this portion of the outlay from their own distribution fee.

Of course, sometimes studios miscalculate and lose money. So do independent production companies, which lack the fee rake-off. And *Sahara* famously lost money—at least for its production company and its owner, billionaire Philip Anschutz. But not for everyone who worked on it. The actors, extras, make-up artists, hair stylists, costumers, assistant directors, set designers, animal wranglers, carpenters, cameramen, grips, editors, musicians, dialogue coaches, sound engineers, caterers, drivers, and publicists all got paid. The stars, director, and writers also got their fixed compensation (though they may never see any part of their contingent compensation, or profit participation). Paramount, which distributed the movie, got its fee. Clive Cussler even got his $10 million. And of course the lawyers on both sides got their fee, as did this expert witness.

PART V

THE NEW STUDIO SYSTEM

THE OSCAR DECEPTION

The 81st Academy Awards, with its scripted speeches by stars, tearful acceptances, eulogies to the rich and the dead, red-carpet celebrity fashion show, and gold-dipped statuettes, had the same mission that the ceremony did when Louis B. Mayer convinced the other studio moguls to create the event in 1927 to "establish the industry in the public's mind as a respectable institution." Now, televised by ABC in dazzling high-definition color, the evening-long informational furthers the long-standing myth that Hollywood is in the business of making great—and original—movies.

This illusion, like all successful deceptions, requires misdirecting the audience's attention from the reality of how Hollywood makes its money to a few brilliant aberrations. Take the 2009 best-picture nominations: *Milk, Frost/Nixon, The Curious Case of Benjamin Button, The Reader,* and *Slumdog Millionaire.* What all these films have in common is that they have little to do with the real business of the Hollywood studios, which is global openings on 3,000 or more screens of youth-oriented movies that, after a few weeks in the multiplexes, can be mass-marketed on DVDs. For the Hollywood elite to choose these atypically adult movies as a public display of its virtue is as absurd as the music industry giving its Grammy Awards to Mozart, Bach, and Verdi or international oil companies presenting awards to avant-garde artists who happen to paint in crude. While Hollywood studios, or their wholly owned—independent—subsidiaries, occasionally make or distribute artistic and social-commentary films, their principal business is no longer about making movies. It is about creating properties—including TV programs, cartoons, videos, and games—that can serve as licensing platforms for a multitude of markets.

The confusion stems from the fact that for the first twenty years of the Academy Awards, the movie business was entirely about movies. But that was before the advent of television, in the late 1940s. The studios simply followed their audiences home. To do this, they first repackaged the movies shown at theaters Pied Piper-style by making movies that visually appealed mainly to children and teenagers and then recycled them into home products, including DVDs, TV shows, games, and toys, which, in 2008, produced some 80 percent of their revenues. In this business model, alas, art, literary, and social-commentary movies are marginalized, since they cannot be either turned into licensing franchises or used to lure huge opening-week audiences to theaters. And, as satisfying as these more artistic films may be to directors, writers, actors, and producers, they do not lend themselves to sequels, prequels, or other licensable properties. They do, however, perform one function very well: acting as decoys at Hollywood's annual celebration of itself.

TEENS AND CAR CRASHES GO TOGETHER

After Hollywood lost its audience to television in the 1950's, it had to reinvent itself. If it could no longer count on habitual moviegoers to fill theaters routinely, it would go into the business of audience-creation. The means studios found to recruit audiences for each and every movie they released was national TV advertising. The tactic that evolved by the 1990s was bombarding a target audience with very expensive thirty-second ads. For this to work, studios had to find a demographic group that was both relatively cheap to reach and who could be induced by this blitz to leave the comfort of their home to see a movie. The audience that satisfied these conditions was teenagers.

Teens have three great advantages over adults for movie studios. First, they tend to predictably cluster around the same TV programs on cable networks, such as MTV, which make them much less costly to reach than moviegoing adults who, if they watch TV at all, tend to be scattered among the most expensive programming in prime time. Second, once in multiplexes, teens tend to consume prodigious quantities of popcorn and soda, which is a powerful attraction to the theater chains that book movies for a wide opening. Third, teens buy electronic games, sports equipment, fast food, and other licensable items, which make them an appealing audience to merchandising partners with the capability of providing the multimillion dollar "tie-in" that help publicize studio movies.

By 2009, studios had become so proficient at finding, activating, and driving the teen herd into multiplexes that over 70 percent of the audience that went to their wide-release movies were under twenty-one years old. Even though the expansion of teen programming on cable and television networks allowed the studios to zero in on their target audience, they needed, as one marketing executive at Sony told me, visuals in a thirty second ad spot that would hook male teens. The movies that filled that bill were action films laden with special effects, explosions, crashes, and mayhem. Sony learned this lesson in June 2003 when it released its action movie *Hollywood Homicide*, with Harrison Ford, a $20 million star, against Universal's action movie *2 Fast 2 Furious*, a lower-budget film without any stars. *Hollywood Homicide* featured images of Harrison Ford in its thirty second ads, whereas *2 Fast 2 Furious* featured flaming car crashes. Even though *Hollywood Homicide* had done much better than *2 Fast 2 Furious* in the pre-openings awareness polls, *2 Fast 2 Furious* had a $50 million opening while *Hollywood Homicide* took in only $11.1 million. The Sony marketing executives could only conclude:

Teens are more excited by car crashes than by big name stars, even one who gets a $20 million dollar paycheck. It thus became as important to cast car crashes and other violent stunts as stars in the teen-oriented remake of Hollywood.

THE STUDIOS—REQUIRED READING

"People of the same trade seldom meet together, even for merriment and diversion, but the conversation ends in a conspiracy against the public, or in some contrivance to raise prices."
—Adam Smith, *The Wealth Of Nations*

In Hollywood, thanks to the services of a secretive research firm called NRG, rival studio executives do not need to meet together and conspire. NRG helps them coordinate openings in such a way that their movies do not compete head-to-head for the same demographic slice of the audience. Founded in 1978 as the National Research Group, NRG—now a part of Nielsen Entertainment—supplies the same weekly "Competitive Positioning" report to each of the six major studios. NRG's founder, Joseph Farrell, signed all of the studios to exclusive contracts, ensuring that the data from his telephone tracking polls became the accepted standard. Because of this monopoly of information, the report provides the studios with a common basis on which to make their scheduling decisions.

Here is how the research is compiled. The NRG telephone pollsters ask a sample of likely moviegoers first whether they are "aware" of a specific movie and, if so, what is the likelihood that they will see it when it opens. They also ask the age and gender of the respondents. The NRG analysts break down the data from these tracking polls into four basic groups, or "quadrants": males under twenty-five, males over twenty-five, females under twenty-five, and females over twenty-five. (In some cases, the respondents are also divided by race.) From these results, NRG projects how well upcoming movies will do against each other in each audience quadrant should they open on the same weekend. For studios, the Competitive Positioning report is critical reading. Why? Nowadays, Hollywood has to create an audience for each and every movie via ad campaigns, appropriately called "drives" (as in "cattle drive"). "If we release twenty-eight films, we need to create twenty-eight different audiences," a Sony marketing executive lamented to me. Audience creation is a hugely expensive exercise. For a drive to work, it must not only round up a herd of moviegoers who favor the movie, it must also get this herd to move at a specific time: opening weekend.

This feat almost invariably requires buying a slew of ads on the limited number of television and cable series that the prospective herd grazes on during the week preceding the opening. To make sure they get the herd's attention, the ads are usually repeated eight times, which is why these drives cost so much. The multimillion-dollar drive runs into a serious problem, however, if a rival studio goes after the same herd that same week— for example, under-twenty-five males—by also buying a parcel of ads on the same shows. The herd then might be cross-pressured and confused, and certainly divided. Such a competition would likely spell failure for both rivals, since even the winner stands to lose a part of the audience to the rival film. To win, then, studios must avoid such conflicts, even if it means yielding to each other.

Enter NRG. The major studios can and do avert such titanic disasters by consulting the NRG Competitive Positioning report. Each studio gets an early warning from the NRG report when one of its films is on a collision course with a competitor's film that appeals to the same herd. By comparing the projected turnouts for both films in the crucial quadrant(s), the studios know which film will lose the matchup, and the losing studio can reschedule its opening to a different weekend, even if it's a less advantageous time period (i.e., not the summer and not the holidays).

Consider how Paramount captured the highly prized Fourth of July weekend in 2005 for *War of the Worlds* even though Warner Bros. had a major contender in *Batman Begins* and 20th Century Fox had *Fantastic Four*. In the NRG tracking polls, all three films did well with males under twenty-five (aka teens), the audience quadrant that's easiest to find clustered around TV programs and, hence, the easiest to stampede toward a July 4 weekend opening. But *War of the Worlds* was also strong in the under-twenty-five female quadrant, so it would easily best both *Batman Begins* and *Fantastic Four*. (In fact, it led in all quadrants.)

Warner Bros. averted a head-to-head competition by opening *Batman Begins* in mid-June, and 20th Century Fox opened *Fantastic Four* on the weekend following July 4. As a result, all three films won their weekend box office and could advertise themselves, as *Fantastic Four* did, as "America's No. 1 hit." No Adam Smith-type conspiratorial meetings were necessary between the rival studio executives of Paramount, Warner Bros., and 20th Century Fox in order to advantageously stagger their film openings so they did not collide. Of course, the weaker contender might try to bluff his way through. For example, in 2002, Disney's subsidiary Miramax had a direct conflict with Dreamworks SKG concerning the openings of their two competing films *Gangs of New York* and *Catch Me If You Can*, both starring Leonardo DiCaprio and both scheduled to open on December 25. Even though the Miramax film had a slightly higher "awareness" level in the targeted males-over-twenty-five audience, Dreamworks refused to yield. At that point, Harvey Weinstein, the president of Miramax, and Jeffrey Katzenberg, a founding partner of Dreamworks SKG, had breakfast in New York to discuss their movies' release dates. As Katzenberg later explained in an interview with the *New York Times*: "He [Weinstein] and I had many conversations about why releasing the movies on the same day was in none of our interest... as both companies have a big investment in Leo DiCaprio." A few days later, Miramax blinked by moving *Gangs of New York* to a different, and less favorable, opening date.

To be sure, NRG's services to the studios go well beyond helping studios avert unpleasant fender benders. It also analyzes much larger issues for the studios, essentially helping them to rethink their entire business models by examining the movies' declining share of the public's "wallet" and "clock" as they compete with music, DVDs, cable TV, downloading, and other forms of home entertainment. But without its Competitive Positioning reports studios would have a much harder time avoiding box office collisions.

THE MIDAS FORMULA

The studios' Midas formula may have been perfected by Steven Spielberg and George Lucas in the 1980s but the innovator was Walt Disney. He put all the elements together back in 1937, when he made *Snow White and the Seven Dwarfs*. The picture was labeled a folly by the moguls who ruled old Hollywood because it was aimed at only a small part of the American audience, children. They were wrong. *Snow White and the Seven Dwarfs*, which was re-released every seven years to a new crop of children, became the first film in history to gross $100 million. It also demonstrated to the studios, among other things, the propensity of children to see the same cartoon over and over again. The movie was also the first to have an official soundtrack, including such songs as "Some Day My Prince Will Come," that became a hit record. More important, *Snow White* had multiple licensable characters (the dwarfs, the wicked witch) who took on long lives of their own, first as toys and later as theme-park exhibits. So, here was Hollywood's future: Its profits would come not from squeezing down the costs of producing films but from creating films with licensable properties that could generate profits in other media over long periods of time.

The advent of computer-based technology has simply provided new ways of mining this vein. The franchises that have raked in over a billion dollars from all markets (including world DVD, television, and toy licensing), *The Lord of the Rings, Harry Potter, Spider-Man, Finding Nemo, Star Wars, Shrek, The Lion King, Toy Story,* and *Pirates of the Caribbean* share most, if not all, of the nine common elements of the Midas formula:

1. They are based on children's fare stories, comic books, serials, cartoons, or, as in the case of *Pirates of the Caribbean*, a theme-park ride.
2. They feature a child or adolescent protagonist (at

least in the establishing episode of the franchise).

3. They have a fairy-tale-like plot in which a weak or ineffectual youth is transformed into a powerful and purposeful hero.

4. They contain only chaste, if not strictly platonic, relationships between the sexes, with no suggestive nudity, sexual foreplay, provocative language, or even hints of consummated passion. (This ensures the movie gets the PG-13 or better rating necessary for merchandising tie-ins and for placing ads on children's TV programming.)

5. They include characters for toy and game licensing.

6. They depict only stylized conflict—though it may be dazzling, large-scale, and noisy, in ways that are sufficiently nonrealistic and bloodless (again allowing for a rating no more restrictive than PG-13).

7. They end happily, with the hero prevailing over powerful villains and supernatural forces (and thus lend themselves to sequels).

8. They use conventional or digital animation to artificially create action sequences, supernatural forces, and elaborate settings.

9. They cast actors who are not ranking stars— at least in the sense that they do not command

dollar-one gross-revenue shares. The success of the DVD has propelled the Midas-formula sequels to dazzlingly high earnings. A studio with a successful franchise now assumes it will sell over 30 million units per sequel, harvesting for itself between $450 million and $600 million dollars. (When *Shrek 2* sold a mere 30 million copies in 2005 and had 7 million in returns— it wiped out a good portion of DreamWorks Animation's quarterly earnings.) While this is an enormously high-stakes game, even a single successful licensing franchise can put a studio in the black—as *Spider-Man* did for Sony Pictures. Midas Formula franchises might not win Oscars, but they keep the studios in business.

YOU CAN'T MAKE MONEY ON MOVIES IN THEATERS

Frank Biondi, who headed two Hollywood studios, Paramount and Universal, told me that the reality of the new studio system is that no studio expects to make money from current production, which is a studio's release of movies to theaters in America. The reason why studios can't make money from their theatrical release is, in a nutshell, that the average cost of luring a customer into a theater is more than they get back from their share of the box office. In 2007, for example, the six major studios spent, on average, $35.9 million for advertising and prints per movie but got back $26.6 million per title. Even if the studios had made the movies for free—which, of course, they didn't (the average cost was $70.9 million)—they would have lost $9.3 million per film on the theatrical run, or "current production."

Why is it so costly to open a movie in multiplexes? Averages, to be sure, can be misleading, especially when, as in this case, adult dramas and comedies are mixed with teenage fantasy and action movies. And despite the average loss, a few films every year, usually franchise installments, such as the latest *Spider-Man*, *Harry Potter*, *Pirates of the Caribbean*, *Batman*, *Lord of the Rings*, and *Shrek*, take in more money than their marketing outlay. Sony's *Spider-Man 3*, for instance, brought in nearly $201 million in rentals—as the distributors' share of the box office is called in the industry—which was more than twice its $88 million advertising and print outlay (the balance of its massive publicity was subsidized, as many franchises are, by toy manufacturers and other merchandising partners). For the vast majority of its films, however, a studio has to look to recoup its losses in later markets on the theory that expending huge sums on its American opening will help the movie wrangle more advantageous play dates in foreign markets, sell more DVDs in video stores, and increase the licensing fees paid by pay-TV. That rationale had merit prior to the digital revolution but nowadays the connection between the American opening and the later markets is much more tenuous.

For one thing, zone-free DVD players, DVD piracy, and Internet file sharing have deeply altered the scenario for foreign distribution. Because movies can now be illegally circulated around the world the instant they open in the United States, the studios have begun to abandon their past practice of staggering foreign openings over many months. As a Fox vice president told *Variety* in 2005, "Waiting three or four months after domestic [release] to release our bigger pictures [overseas] is not something we can do anymore." The result is more and more simultaneous openings in the US box office since figures come too late to help get better foreign play.

As for DVDs a handful of mass marketers, such as Wal-Mart, now account for most of the studios' revenues, and these retailers demand, and get, a separate marketing campaign, often costing

$15-20 million per title, aimed at their customers, and not only teen movie audiences. After all, unlike other stores, the big retailers view DVDs as traffic-builders, as one Wal-Mart executive put it, aimed at bringing in the relatively well-heeled, plasma-screen-purchasing customers, not the so-called LICs (or low-income consumers). As a rueful Sony marketing executive pointed out, "Unfortunately, our teens are not always who they want."

This disconnect leaves Hollywood in a bind. A studio needs to create audiences for its entire slate of movies to maintain good will with the multiplex chains and to find the franchises that are immensely profitable, which means it will almost ineluctably lose money on its current production. But, always resourceful, Hollywood has found out a way to mitigate its losses on the adult dramas, comedy, and other non-franchise material: it sells a share of them to outside investors.

THE FOREIGN MIRAGE

When Hollywood movies fail to find audiences in America, it is often claimed that these movies redeem their losses overseas. The assumption here is

THE RISE OF THE HOME ENTERTAINMENT ECONOMY

Worldwide MPAA Studio Receipts
(Inflation-corrected, 2007 US Dollars)
Billions of dollars
Inflation-Adjusted in 2003 Dollars

Year	Theat-rical	Video/DVD	TV (including pay-TV, PPV)	Total	Theatrical as % of Total Revenue
1948	8.5	0	0	8.5	100
1980	4.9	2.2	4.1	9.22	55
1985	3.3	2.6	7.4	13.3	25
1990	6.8	6.5	10.1	22.4	22
1995	6.2	11.9	11.6	29.7	19.6
2000	6.5	13.1	15.5	35.1	19.4
2003	8.7	21.1	18.7	48.5	17.9
2004	8.1	22.8	18.1	49	16.9
2005	7	22.6	16.9	46.5	15.1
2006	8.2	19.8	16.1	44.1	18.5
2007*	8.8	17.9	16.2	42.9	20.4

*The studios stopped furnishing these revenue numbers to the MPA in 2008.

that the box office receipts abroad are pure gravy for the movie studios. For example, the usually financially-savvy *Wall Street Journal* reported on November 19, 2004, that three notable "duds" in America— *Troy*, *The Terminal*, and *King Arthur*—"ended up turning handsome profits" because "in each case, box office receipts from outside the US far outweighed domestic returns." It then cited impressive sounding numbers: *Troy* "made" $363 million internationally; *The Terminal*, $96.3 million internationally; and *King Arthur*, $149.8 million abroad—as if these receipts represented their salvation.

In reality, however, these impressive-sounding receipts represented the foreign theaters' revenue, not the studios' share of them. In fact, the studios get an even smaller share of the foreign than of the American box office. In 2007, the studios' share averaged about 40 percent of ticket sales. And from those revenues, studios have to pay for foreign advertising, prints, taxes, insurance, translations, etc. Once those expenses are deducted, the studios are lucky to wind up with 15 percent of what is reported as the foreign gross.

Consider, Disney's *Gone in 60 Seconds*. Its reported "foreign gross" was $129,477,395. Of that sum, Disney got $55,979.966, of which it paid out $37,986,053 in expenses.

They included:

Foreign Advertising	$25,197,723
Foreign Prints	$ 5,660,837
Foreign Taxes	$ 5,077,286
Foreign Versions	$ 822,997
Foreign Shipping	$ 454,973
Currency Conversion	$ 266,900
Foreign Trade Dues	$ 122,275

After paying these expenses, Disney was left with just $17,993,913—a far cry from the reported $129,477,395 "gross." And the film is still over $153 million in the red. So while the foreign box office helps, it does not necessarily make a movie profitable.

THE QUEST FOR THE DIGITALIZED COUCH POTATO

The numbers—or at least the secret studio revenue numbers in the May 2008 *All Media Revenue Report*—tell the story. As late as 1980, movie theaters provided the studios with 55 percent of their total revenues; in 2007, movie theaters provided only 20 percent of their total revenue (over half of which came from overseas). The other 80 percent now came from the ubiquitous couch potato who was viewing his movies at home via DVDs, Blu-rays, pay-per-view, a digital recorder, cable channels, or even network television. A studio's task in this new environment, as Sony Chairman Howard Stringer explained to me, "is to optimally leverage our product across all these [new] platforms." The way studios achieve this "optimal leverage" is to give each of these platforms a discreet time frame, or window in which it could exploit the home audience.

A brief history is in order. Since the 1980s, the studios have managed their revenue by employing a system of "windows" to release their products to different markets. First, movies play in theaters, then, six months later, the video window opens, followed by the opening of the pay-TV and then free television window.

Then at the turn of the millennium the prospect of mass sales of DVDs in retail stores began opening cracks in the entire system. Warner Bros. led the way. To win critical shelf space in Wal-Marts, they needed to release their summer blockbusters such as *Harry Potter* and *Batman* on DVD during the hottest sales periods, Thanksgiving to Christmas, instead of waiting for an artificial window to open up later. So they shortened their window. Other studios followed suit with a vengeance, shrinking the window to four, or in some cases even three, months. Then thanks to the Internet, studios began to announce an upcoming DVD while the movie was still playing in theaters. As a top studio executive explained to me, "It was a voluntary decision made for purely financial reasons by the major players... to satisfy quarterly profit goals, nothing more, nothing less." To avoid losing audiences, multiplex chains, which need to maximize their popcorn sales to stay in business, cut the run of such movies. The consequence was a spiral that fed on itself: the shorter the run, the less money from the box office. This decrease, in turn, further increased pressure from the young Turks in the studios's home-entertainment divisions to further collapse the window. The main resistance to this change came from the old-guard studio executives who fear that undercutting the movie-theater business will—even if it improves DVD sales—unravel the very foundations of Hollywood. They argued that the theatrical platform, to which most of the PR hoopla, magazine covers, TV talk shows, and the rest of the celebrity-worshiping culture is geared, is crucial to generate worldwide DVD sales.

Amidst this battle to devise a strategy for the DVD window, the entire window system began to disintegrate as digital downloading and other new forms of delivery threatened to make irrelevant the artificial boundaries between pay-TV, network television and cable television. The $64 billion question for the studios is now: Does any barrier, no less a fragile window, make sense in the quest for the couch potato in an increasingly digital age?

UNORIGINAL SIN

In Hollywood, originality is anything but a virtue. Paramount rejected a recent project that had attached stars, an approved script, and a bankable director by telling the producer: "It's a terrific idea, too bad it has not been made into a movie already or we could have done the remake." This response, alas, is not untypical. Studios today, as a former executive explained, tend to green-light four types of movies for wide openings: remakes (such as *King Kong*), sequels (such as *Star Wars: Episode III*), television spin-offs (such as *Mission: Impossible*), or video game extensions (such as *Lara Croft: Tomb Raider*).

If Hollywood is originality-challenged, it is not because studio executives find particular joy in mindlessly imitating bygone successes, or lack imagination. It is because they must take into account the underlying reality of today's entertainment economy. In the prior system (1928-1950) each studio, was identified with a particular genre of movies: MGM (musicals and romantic comedies); Paramount (historical epics); Warner Bros. (gangster stories); 20th Century Fox (social dramas); Universal (horror movies); Disney (cartoons), and just the mention of a studio star like Clark Gable or Carole Lombard on a marquee was enough to guarantee a full house. To this end, a studio could rely on a vast habitual herd of moviegoers, to go to the movies in an average week. Most of these people went to see not just a new movie— the main attraction—but also a program of weekly entertainment that included newsreels, a slapstick short, a cliffhanger serial, a "B" feature, such as a Western, and needed no national advertising to prod it. That was before TV provided an alternative source of entertainment.

Today is a different story. The studio names mean little, if anything at all, to audiences. Nor can the weekly audience, which has shrunk to less than 10 percent of the population, be relied on to show up for any particular movie. Studios must therefore create audiences from scratch for each and every film. For the studios, "audience creation" has become just as important a creative product as the film itself.

These multiplex owners know that the six major studios can supply not only a movie, but the publicity campaign capable of driving a herd of moviegoers from their homes to the theater on an opening weekend. The studios have this capacity because, unlike independent film producers, they control when, where, and how the movie will be released, starting from the day it goes into production. With this control, the studios can shape the movie to fit the requisites of the marketing campaign, fusing both product and publicity, like Siamese twins, into a single entity. This carefully calibrated movie product can then be used to recruit multimillion-dollar merchandising tie-ins, such as with McDonald's. The studios can also insert "teasers" in the coming-attraction reels (which they control) to build audience awareness. Finally, the studios have the resources to commit up to $50 million in prerelease advertising on a single movie.

The marketing campaign has become crucial for theater owners because the names of big stars can no longer be relied on to draw a large audience unless it is incorporated into a studio-sized marketing campaign. Consider two consecutive romantic comedies with Julia Roberts, one of the highest-paid actresses; one an independent release, the other a studio release. The first, *Everyone Says I Love You*, released by Miramax, brought in $132,000 on its opening weekend. The second, *My Best Friend's Wedding*, released by Sony, brought in $21.7 million in its opening weekend. Both films had the same star actress, same genre, same romantic twist, but one film drew 150 times as many people to theaters as the other. Next, consider two consecutive movies starring Mel Gibson. The first, *What Women Want*, was released by Paramount and brought in $33.6 million in its opening weekend, while the second, *Million Dollar Hotel*, released three months later by Lion's Gate, brought in $29,483. A thousand times as many people went to see the opening of the studio product, although both starred Gibson. Even if Roberts' *Everyone Says I Love You* and Gibson's *Million Dollar Hotel* had been vastly superior movies to their studio counterparts (and I believe they were), the results would have been the same. These films played in only a handful of theaters, while *My Best Friend's Wedding* opened on 2,134 screens and *What Women Want* opened on 3,013 screens. For the independent films to have opened "wide" as their studio counterparts did, the distributors would have had to convince the theater chains that they had the wherewithal to provide the kind of massive marketing campaign that it takes to fill 2,000 theaters with popcorn-eating audiences—a next-to-impossible undertaking.

But, unlike its movies, the ending is not a happy one for originality. Since the publicity campaigns for these blockbusters have proven effective in the popcorn economy, studios recycle their elements into endless sequels, such as those for *Spider-Man, Pirates of the Caribbean, Shrek*, and *Mission Impossible*, which then become the studios' franchises on which they earn almost all their profits. That is their unoriginal sin and, alas, salvation in the new system.

THE SAMURAI EMBRACE

The momentous shift from theaters to homes proceeded from a series of decisions made not in Hollywood or New York, but in Tokyo and Osaka.

This reinvention of the film business began in the 1970s with the engineering by Sony and Matsushita of an affordable videocassette recorder. Through a process of ingenious compromises, Sony made its Betamax small enough to fit on top of a TV set and foolproof enough to be operated by a child. The Hollywood studios led by Universal fought for seven years in the courts to prevent it from reaching the market.

If they had prevailed over Sony, the video rental market may never have developed, but, fortunately for the studios, they lost their case in the Supreme Court in 1984. (It was a bittersweet victory for Sony who, in the interim, lost the format war to the even more user-friendly VHS format developed by Matsushita.)

The VCR soon became a ubiquitous household appliance, video stores became a part of the urban landscape and the newfound flow of money from video rentals proved to be financial salvation for the very studios that had so bitterly fought the new technology. As a consequence, in deciding what films to make, studios approved projects that had greater potential for huge video rentals. These proved to be special-effects laden disaster and fantasy films that appealed to children and teenagers. Films that did not fit the requisites of video buyers were given a lower priority and, as it turned out, these included dramas, comedies and political exposés intended for an older, more diverse, and less predictable audience.

Next, in the mid-1990s, Toshiba and Sony changed the Hollywood equation even more radically by substituting a digital platform the "DVD" for the videocassette. As with the VCR, this digital future was resisted by most of the Hollywood studios who were concerned that it might kill the video business that had become their golden goose. But now Sony, which owned the Columbia Tristar studio, and Toshiba, which was a part owner (and strategic partner) of the Warner Bros. studio, had marshaled enough power in Hollywood to ensure that enough titles would be available for the DVD launch. The combined libraries of these two studios included over 24,000 titles. So, in August 1995, in a conference in Hawaii, Sony and Toshiba (and all the other Japanese manufacturers) agreed on a single format.

Even though most of the other major studios did not participate, the DVD roll-out succeeded in transforming films into a retail product. DVDs could be played not only on DVD players, but on personal computers, game consoles, iPods, and other digital devices. By 2000, Wal-Mart had become Hollywood's single biggest customer, selling about a third of all DVDs, occasioning top studio executives to journey to Bentonville, Arkansas, to find out what ratings, stars, genres, and other attributes would help them win strategic placement in Wal-Mart stores.

Throughout the 1990s studios had been cutting back on the number of titles they released since the popcorn culture at the multiplexes did not require much diversity. But now retailers such as Wal-Mart, Target, and Borders allocated valuable shelf space according to the numbers of titles a studio could deliver. As shelf space became the new name of the game, studios sought to increase their leverage, or throw weight, by buying up independent distributors (and later "mini-majors") to get more titles. As a result, six companies—Time Warner, Sony, Fox, Viacom, Disney, and Universal—came to dominate not only all the major releases but the entire universe of so-called indie releases. The DVD, with its random access and easy navigation, also opened up for these companies a rich new market: boxed sets of TV series. Not only could they tap their huge TV libraries, but they could invest in original series, such as *The Sopranos, Mad Men, Big Love, The Wire, Rome, Dexter, Sex and the City*, and *24*, which often proved more profitable than films that opened in theaters.

For the growing home audience, the DVD also made films a more interactive experience. Couch potatoes could now change the language of a film, its aspect ratio, rating, or ending; watch additional scenes (which in some cases are shot for the DVD), or listen to commentaries by directors, writers, and actors, or play a game, music video, or gag reel. With these bonus features driving a large part of DVD sales—one-third of polled DVD buyers said that they first played the bonus feature—Hollywood's films became part of a package.

The next move by the Japanese electronic giants came in 2005: the high-definition disc. Pioneered by Japanese television in the late 1970s, high definition makes the home the equivalent of a theater by furnishing film-like images on a large screen. There were two versions, Toshiba's HD-DVD and Sony's Blu-ray.

Since both render a similar quality image, the battle between Sony and Toshiba turned on who could enroll Hollywood studios in support of their format. And, as the Japanese manufacturers knew from their past format wars, this would require bribes in the form of "replication deals." Sony had an advantage in that it owned one of the major studios, Sony Pictures. It then bought control of MGM—almost exclusively for the purpose of locking its library into the Blu-ray formula. And it made secret deals with Disney and Fox, giving it four studios with about half of Hollywood's desirable titles. Toshiba fought back by spending over a quarter of billion dollars in cash replication deals, getting for its money Paramount, Universal, and Dreamworks to commit to exclusively put their titles on Toshiba's HD-DVD format. The format war was then decided by Warner Bros., which sold almost 40 percent of all DVDs. Its new CEO, Jeff Bewkes, decided its interest lay in establishing a single format, and opted for Blu-ray.

Meanwhile, Sony launched PlayStation 3, which despite its juvenile sounding name, is a state-of-the-art computer that can connect wirelessly to TV sets, computers, printers, and the Internet, and simultaneously run up to nine different kinds of consumer electronics, play and record high-definition films, download movies from the Internet and (with a card) cable television, and, as far as games go, render characters in frighteningly realistic ways. The result is further convergence of Hollywood's dream factory with the digital domain.

The hand of Tokyo may not always be visible in the dazzling glitter of Hollywood, but it has enabled it to re-invent itself. It is not that the Japanese set out to change the way the world sees movies, it is that Hollywood failed to see its own digital destiny.

DOWNLOADING FOR DOLLARS

Up until 2007, the studio's principal access to the home market came through pay-TV, free television, video rentals, and DVD sales. But now, with products such as Apple's video iPod and TiVo-type digital recorders becoming widely available, Hollywood is inching towards an even more lucrative way of exploiting the home market.

Disney's ABC network, for example, made a deal with Apple that will allow iPod users to download and watch shows for $1.99 an episode. The other networks, CBS, which is still controlled by Sumner Redstone, and NBC, a subsidiary of NBC Universal, are selling their programs for 99 cents a viewing via linkups with cable and satellite providers.

This downloading strategy is particularly appealing to the broadcast networks because, unlike cable networks, broadcast networks presently get no cash compensation from cable operators. (At best, cable operators might agree to carrying their new cable networks.) But by offering their hit programs for downloading the next day, networks get cash from the cable audience. A cost of 99 cents a pop is hardly trivial when multiplied by a cable audience of thirty or so million. The downside is that they may lose part of their regular TV viewers, and the advertising revue that goes with their loyalty. But the networks are betting that their regular audience, which can watch the programs free, would have little incentive to wait a day and download them for a fee. Even Netflix, which has been enormously successful using the mail to deliver rental DVDs for a monthly fee, has now created an online delivery system to replace trips to the post office.

The studios stand to gain even more from a huge audience willing to pay to download movies from their libraries. Unlike DVDs or Blu-rays, which require manufacturing, warehousing, distribution, and disposing of returns, it costs almost nothing to download a movie or cartoon. Indeed, all of the costs of transmission would be borne by the cable operator (or a site like the Apple iTunes Store), whose cut would be less, under present arrangements, than retailers get on DVDs. So if a movie were a huge hit, such as *Shrek*, and millions of orders flooded in, the marginal cost of filling them would be near zero. The consumer, once he bought the download, could watch it where and when he chose to, just as he once watched a DVD.

The real issue for the Hollywood studios is how they can dig into this potential gold mine without undermining their existing revenue streams.

With the possibility of costlessly providing millions of downloads to consumers of both their older and new films, the studio heads, including Disney's Robert Iger, are openly discussing a radical revamping of the window system. Obviously, if a home download of a movie were available at the same time (and price) as its DVD release, the download option might replace retail sales. To avoid that outcome, and a potentially dangerous confrontation with Wal-Mart, the studios would have to delay the download release until well after the DVD release. But while the studios may find this embarrassment of choices somewhat paralyzing at present, as more and more consumers get digital recorders or video iPods, downloading for dollars may prove irresistible.

EPILOGUE

THE END OF THE BEGINNING— OR THE END?

HOLLYWOOD: THE MOVIE

Hollywood has spent the better part of the last
century making movies out of the great inspira-
tional sagas of human history. Ironically, the one
epic it has yet to make is one about a uniquely
American achievement that has and continues to
mesmerize the world: The Rise of Hollywood.
Here is a true *Sturm und Drang* melodrama, full of
fascinating characters from the edges who overcome seemingly impossible obstacles to build a

new industry that today defines the world of mass entertainment. The scenario would follow the classic Hollywood three-act formula.

ACT ONE

Fade in on the men who founded the studios of Hollywood. These are self-made and self-educated Jewish immigrants from European ghettoes, who, before they got into the movie business, had been ragpickers, furriers, errand boys, butchers, and junk peddlers. They are true outliers: men like Louis B. Mayer, Samuel Goldwyn, Jack Warner, Adolph Zucker, William Fox, Carl Laemmle, and Harry Cohn, who first scraped together money to build arcades and nickelodeons to show movies, then resourcefully expanded into theater circuits, using bicyclists to deliver reels between their theaters. As movies become a national craze, they build distribution networks to service other exhibitors, and then studios to assure that they have enough movies. Along the way, they battle part of the establishment in the form of the powerful Edison Trust, which, aside from its patents on electricity generation, holds numerous patents on movie cameras and projectors. When "the Trust," as it is ominously known, attempts to use the courts in New York and Massachusetts to take over the movie business, the movie-makers move their studios to the newly incorporated village of Hollywood, a place they can control and build. By the mid-1920s, 57 million people—over half the population—are going to their movies every week. Yet the saga is just beginning. In 1927, sound comes to the movies. After audiences are mesmerized by Al Jolson in *The Jazz Singer*, Hollywood, in one of the great technological feats of modern history, converts most of the 21,000 movie theaters in America to sound and turns their studios into sound stages. The studios create new galaxies of stars for their talkie movies. Despite even the great depression of the 1930s, the weekly audience grows to 75 million, who go to their neighborhood theaters not just to see feature movies, but newsreels, comedy shorts, action-packed serials, and cartoons. A new generation of talent, including such brilliant innovators as Walt Disney, expands its realm to children's entertainment, and color adds to its ability to entertain the public even in the bleak years of the Depression and the grim war years of the early 1940s.

ACT TWO

The Second World War has ended, the troops have come home. By 1948, the studio system is at its zenith. More than 90 million Americans—two-thirds of the population—go to the movies on a weekly basis. The studios produce more than 500 feature movies per year, have all the major stars under iron-clad contract, and employ more than 320,000 people. Their illusion-making technology is unmatched anywhere in the world. In little more than a generation, its founders have literally gone from rags to riches. The studio heads, now called "moguls" after Oriental potentates, are among the highest-paid executives in the world.

But a new invention is casting an ever-darkening cloud: television. Even with its fuzzy black-and-white pictures, it offers nearly free stay-at-home entertainment, which gradually captures a larger and larger portion of the studios' habitual audience. In addition, a long-simmering antitrust action severs the studios' hold on American theaters. According to the consent decree they sign, they must divest themselves of the theaters they own and give up their practice of forcing independently owned theaters to book an entire package of movies if they want any at all. The final blow to the studio system comes when stars, at the behest of their newly empowered agents, refuse to sign long-term contracts. The moguls now have to compete with independent and foreign producers for both theater bookings and stars.

After color TV is introduced in the 1950s, the movies' weekly audience goes into free fall. By 1958, it is less than half the size of the 1948 audience. Drive-ins, Cinemascope, 3-D, Surround Sound, and other innovations fail to win back the audience from television. The entertainment landscape in America has changed, and reflecting this change, the stock prices of studios plummet to levels not seen since the Great Depression. Prophets of doom predict that the end of Hollywood is near.

ACT THREE

However, the prophets have underestimated Hollywood's resourcefulness. For a half-century, its genius has been its ability to adapt to new circumstances. It is, after all, in the business of entertaining mass audiences, and those audiences, though diverted, have not vanished. So Hollywood reinvents itself. The old studio system, with its contractual control of theaters and stars, is dead; long live the new studio system. Unable to depend on a habitual weekly audience that has defected to television, it turns television to its own advantage by using national TV advertising to create tailor-made audiences for each and every movie. It greatly expands its reach overseas, creating a second stream of revenue from theaters and television abroad.

Nor does the new Hollywood limit itself to theaters. It finds new sources of revenue in licensing its movies to television, originating prime-time series, renting its movies on home video, putting them on planes and in hotels, reincarnating their characters as toys, and then, with the digital revolution, putting its movies on DVDs, Blu-ray discs, video-on-demand, cell phones, and the Internet. Since networks are restricted by a Federal Communication Commission rule from having a financial interest in their programming, the studios become the main suppliers of prime-time television (which they could later sell to local stations). This expansion not only keeps the movie business alive, it makes it central to the world's entertainment economy. But beyond the movies, the money, and the job creation, Hollywood produces another form of wealth: the pictures in our head by which the world at large defines the phenomenon of American culture. What a movie that achievement would make.

ARE INDIE MOVIES DEAD?

"Dear Hollywood Economist," an anonymous producer based in Paris wrote me on my website in

December 2009. "I am trying to raise $20 million through pre-sales for my next movie. So far I have had no success. A former Miramax executive, who is now in the business herself of arranging financing for independent movies, told me 'the indie business is all but dead.' Is she right?"

The answer, alas, is that the indie financier is essentially correct. The hoary game of using foreign pre-sales to finance the production of American films, which was pioneered by the Italian impresario Dino Di Laurentiis in the 1970s, is now nearly over. It involved using what were essentially promissory notes from foreign distributors as collateral to borrow the funds necessary to make a movie. Here is how it is (or was) played.

First, an indie producer assembles a script, director, and stars acceptable to a "territorial buyer." The most important territorial buyers are distributors in Germany, France, Italy, Britain, Spain, and Japan. Then he signs a contract giving the buyer theatrical, DVD and TV rights to the territory in return for an agreed-upon sum to be paid at a future date when the completed film is delivered. Ideally, the foreign buyer also provides an assignable letter of credit that will become effective on delivery. The producer repeats this process with other foreign buyers for different territories until he has enough paper commitments to finance the movie. But before he can monetize them, he also needs to get a completion bond, backed by an insurer, that guarantees that the film will be completed with stars and other essential elements specified in the contracts. This requires the producer furnishing a budget to a completion bond company and accepting its conditions. Finally, he goes to a bank with the completion bond and the contracts and borrows the money covered by the pre-sales agreement. The bank takes only a limited risk since if the film is not completed and delivered, it is repaid by the completion bond company, and if delivered, it is repaid by proceeds from the letters of credit from the foreign buyers. So it deducts the pre-paid interest and other banking fees, and gives the producer the balance. As complex and time-consuming as the process is—it can take years to complete—these pre-sales had been the mainstay of the indie industry for three decades up until 2008. Then came the perfect storm.

First, DVD sales fell by more than 20 percent in all the major pre-sales markets in 2008, and even more in 2009. Given this trend, the foreign buyers realized that they could no longer rely on DVD revenues in the future to make up the gap in their commitments. To make their situation even worse, television stations in Europe, which had been the largest buyers of movie rights in Europe, found their budgets constrained by the financial crisis and severely cut back on their future purchases. On top of these problems, the rapid expansion of broadband in Europe and Asia greatly increased the ease of digital downloading. Since many of these territories opened films many months after the American release, the availability of pirated versions threatened to undercut the stream of revenues from theaters. As a top executive of a French distributor said, "Why should we buy in advance the exclusive rights to a movie when our potential customers can download it before we can release it?"

Further dampening these foreign buyers appetite for making pre-sale deals was the failure of indie films to get distribution in America (which they often depended on to generate publicity for their release). As one indie producer wrote me "foreign distributors tend to buy films that have meaningful US muscle behind them," but by the time she arrived at the Cannes festival in 2008 to look for such deals, five major US distributors for indie films— New Line Cinema, Fine Line Features, Picturehouse, Warner Independent Films, and Paramount Vantage—announced they were closing, while others, such as the Weinstein Company, said they were running out of money. By November 2009, the situation grew even gloomier, with Miramax announcing it was closing its main office in New York. The bottom line for foreign buyers is that many of the movies being offered to them for pre-sales after 2010 may never have a major opening—or publicity blitz—in America.

The coup de grace may have been the global financial crisis. Some banks, whose balance sheets were hurt by bad debt, such as Deutsche Bank, closed down their film financial units and others now insisted on far more strenuous, and onerous, terms to finance pre-sales. One indie producer based in New York complained, "Even if one can find pre-sale deals it is now almost impossible to get money. The banks that used to lend us money against these licensing contracts are now demanding written guarantees from the territorial buyer that they will be paid even if the movie is not delivered." To get a foreign buyer to agree to such terms—which in effect makes him responsible for the completion bond—would require further concessions by the producer. Moreover, each new turn of the screw by banks escalates the producer's legal costs, especially if they are billed by the hour. According to the New York producer, his transaction costs for pre-sale deals both in terms of time and money have now risen to the point that "they no longer make financial sense."

This confluence has left indie movies in a dire situation. Nevertheless, in the curious mirror world of Hollywood, hope springs eternal, even if it comes in the form of a rich relative, Chinese tycoon, or Indian industrialist entranced with a movie fantasy. While studios are increasingly concentrating their energies on comic book sequels, indie producers have shown great resourcefulness in exploiting original ideas, such as *Slumdog Millionaire*. All they need is to find a new strategy for financing their alternative to Hollywoood.

THE RISE OF THE TUBE MOGULS

In the new millennium, Robert Iger, former head of ABC television, got Michael Eisner's spot at Disney. Brad Grey, the former head of a television production company, Brillstein Grey Entertainment, became the studio head at Paramount. Howard Stringer, a former president of CBS Television, became the first non-Japanese chairman of Sony. Peter Chernin, a former president of Fox broadcasting, became chairman of the Fox Entertainment Group, which includes the Twentieth-Century Fox studio. Robert C. Wright, the former head of NBC television, became head of NBC Universal, which owns the Universal studio. And Jeff Bewkes, the head of HBO, became chairman of Time Warner. That all of Hollywood's new moguls have come from the

realm of television reflects a singular if dismal reality: in 2009, only about 2 percent of Americans
went to the movies on a given day, whereas more
than 90 percent of them watched something on
television at home. What used to be a business centered in movie houses has been transformed into a
one centered around TVs and computers. In 1948,
ticket sales from theaters provided all the studios'
revenues; in 2007, theaters in the United States and
aboard accounted for just over 20 percent of the
take. Instead, home entertainment provided nearly
80 percent of the revenue.

Moreover, the shift to home entertainment is
gathering momentum as couch potatoes find more
convenient ways to obtain movies in a high-definition format, such as Netflix (which by 2009 had
streamed more than 1 billion movies) and cheaper
rentals, such the vending machines of Redbox,
which in 2009 offered them at 99 cents per night
and accounted for almost one-third of DVD rentals. Since the average ticket at the multiplex costs
over $7, this new 99-cent rental price could in-
duce more and more people to skip the theater.
Of course, there will always be a niche audience
for movie theaters, if only among teens who want
to get out of their homes on weekends, but that
niche will not be a significant profit center for
the new Hollywood. Already, theatrical releases,

despite the blinding allure they still hold for the media, serve essentially as launching platforms for videos, DVDs, network TV, pay-TV, games, and a host of other products.

This transformation is not necessarily bad news for Hollywood's big six studios. Ever since the 1970s, they have produced the largest share of television's most successful series, including such hits as the various *CSI* shows. Their immense libraries syndicate or license to cable networks and local station most of their movies and television shows, and they earn a royalty from each movie sent out at Netflix, as well as licensing fees on moves rented at Blockbuster and other video-store chains. Even Redbox pays the studio the same wholesale price as other video stores (about 65 percent of the retail price). Consequently, it isn't surprising that the studios are now promoting executives who are more experienced with the mass audience than with the vanishing movie-theater audience.

TRADING ANALOG DOLLARS FOR DIGITAL PENNIES

In early 2008, a top studio executive, discussing the previous year's revenue numbers, said, 'Who in their right mind would swap these analog dollars for digital pennies?" The "analog dollars" he went over with me were indeed impressive. They came from DVDs (though they are not analog products), pay television, cable and network television, local stations, and licensing products. The "digital pennies" he referred to came mainly from downloading from Amazon Video on Demand, the Apple iTunes Store, and other websites. Since most of the audience still watched their movies on TV sets rather than on their computers, he saw little reason for the studios to jettison what in the past ten years had proved to be a highly lucrative business model for a nebulous one. The studios' 2007 number powerfully supported his point. The six major studios' "analog dollars" amounted to $42.9 billion, with $8.8 billion coming from theaters, $16.2 billion coming from pay and free television, and $17.9 billion from DVDs. That year, the studios' "digital dollars" from downloads amounted to less than $400 million.

Less than two years later, this same top executive had radically revised his thinking. He said that the home TV sets on which 100 million Americans watched the studios' movies, either on DVDs, pay-TV, or free-TV, would soon act as computers. The "tipping point" will come as new sets allow the audience to surf the web with their remote control. By the end of 2010, almost all major TV manufacturers in Japan, Korea, and China will equip their sets with this technology. At the very minimum, this development will mean that the TV audience will have at their fingertips an immense amount of non-Hollywood product. Consider that in 2009 alone, YouTube streamed more than 9 billion videos; Hulu, a service that did not even exist in 2007, sent TV programs to 35 million computers, and Microsoft's Xbox, Sony's PlayStation, and other game machines had 40 million users. Clearly, as couch potatoes become websurfers Hollywood will have to compete with all this material for their limited time, or "clock."

Even more threatening, the TV-as-computer hybrid will give the entire home audience far easier access to pirated versions of Hollywood's movies and TV programs. For most of the twentieth century, Hollywood could control its movies because it had a tangible product: reels of film that it could deliver and retrieve from theaters. But the digital revolution changed everything. Movies now can be distributed by a digital formula. And from those ones and zeroes, the movie can be reconstructed in perfect fidelity by a tiny computer chip. Even with the support of governments, private detective agencies, and armies of litigators, the studios have found it difficult if not impossible to quash the copying of these digitalized formulae over the Internet. Each effort to suppress them has led to more ingenious ways to share them. Consider, for example, the recent spread of "cyber-lockers," which are essentially online storage sites. They hold a large number of movie-sized files that can be downloaded by anyone who has been given, or bought, a password. Because the studios' enforcement agents cannot ascertain the contents of these lockers without the passwords, the lockers are almost impossible to police. Compounding the problem, the hosts are often located in countries outside the purview of American or European copyright laws. As a Warner Bros. technical operations chief explained in 2008, many now serve as "facilitators to access pirated content."

Such piracy cuts directly to the heart of the studios' current practice of staggering the release of their products over a long period—the so-called "windows" system. As Howard Stringer, the chairman of Sony, explained to me, studios depend for their profits on their ability to "optimally leverage" their movies in these different media markets. So after the multiplexes play a movie, it is released first in video stores, then on pay-TV channels such as HBO, Showtime, and Starz, and later on free and cable television. Thus each market gets an exclusive window for its version of the movie. But if the vast home audience can get immediate access via downloads from cyber-lockers and other Internet sources, the exclusivity loses its value, and the entire window system cracks. Why should HBO pay $15 million for rights to an exclusive window for the latest Harry Potter movie when its viewers can download it from the Internet?

By 2009, the handwriting was on Hollywood's wall: its windows could not be kept open in an age in which its crown jewels—movies—could be perfectly replicated on a computer. One alternative would be for Hollywood to attempt to protect the windows by stamping out digital piracy. Such a feat would require not only the cooperation of authorities in every country that could host a website or cyber-locker, but a global campaign to change the values of users who see nothing wrong with sharing digital downloads. Another alternative would be to abandon the windows system and attempt to preempt the effects of digital piracy by releasing movies almost simultaneously to multiplexes, video stores, download services, and television. One top Paramount strategist foresees a scenario in which, after multiplexes are converted to digital projection, "a movie opens on 25,000 screens around the world in a single weekend, and within a week it's available for downloads, Netflix, video stores, and cable tele vision." This would allow the ad campaign—and its word-of-mouth—to promote it in any form that anyone is willing to pay for. Such a drastic remedy could not help but affect which films the movie studios produce, since to activate the interest in a global mass audience, new movies will require universally appealing elements (action, graphic content) and easily comprehended themes.

Hollywood, to be sure, is not a single entity. Between them, the big six studios—Disney, Fox, Time Warner, Viacom, Universal NBC, and Sony—control almost all movie distribution in the United States. Their corporate parents have very different interests. Universal NBC, for example, makes most of its money from its ownership of television and cable networks, whereas Sony, which owns no television networks, make a large part of its money from manufacturing digital hardware, including its PlayStation 3, DVD players, and high-definition televisions. These companies also have very different leadership styles. But even if they wanted to collude on their responses to the digital challenges—or on the pricing of downloads and DVDs—they would be prohibited from doing so by both American and European antitrust laws. Perhaps they will fare better than their counterparts in the music business did in suppressing digital copying; if they don't, they will almost certainly suffer a similar withering-away of the "analog dollars" that flow in through their staggered windows. The separations between these windows will make less and less sense, and at some point, one studio owner—my candidate is Rupert Murdoch—will decide to break with the status quo and move toward the alternative of simultaneous releases. Others will then follow right on his heels. Hollywood will swap its vaunted analog dollars for digital pennies, but it may well discover that there are billions of those pennies out there.

APPENDIX

WARNER BROS DISTRIBUTION
REPORT #6
Midnight In The Garden of Good Evil,
September 30, 2007

This report reflects the financial status of the 1997 movie *Midnight In The Garden of Good Evil* eighty-seven months after its release, a span long enough to reflect TV licensing and other back-end revenue. Based on the hugely successful novel by John Berendt, it was directed by Oscar winning director Clint Eastwood, and starred Jude Law, Kevin Spacey, and John Cusack.

1. "Defined Gross" is a term of art in Hollywood accounting used to avoid any confusion or litigation over what is meant by "Gross." In the case of everything but video, it is the total revenues that are received from all sources. In the case of video (which includes both VHS and DVD), it is a royalty, which, in this case, is 20 percent of wholesale sales.

2. "Fee" refers to the fee taken by the distributors, Warner Bros. Pictures and Warner Home Video,

both of which are wholly-owned subsidiaries of Time Warner, which financed the movie.

3. The advertising and publicity expense of $33.8 million and the print cost of $3.4 million include foreign as well as domestic costs.

4. "Residual Payments" include the fixed amount deducted from television licensing for pension plans. This applies to every film made with union labor (which is virtually every studio-made movie in the world).

5. "The Defined Proceeds," in this case a deficit, is $85.5 million. This includes interest of $22.7 million, which is a notional charge (though studios do pay interest on their lines of credit).

6. "Negative cost" refers to investment in the film itself. It includes above-the-line expenses, such as the money paid for the book, script, producer, director, and principal actors, and the below-the-line costs, which include daily shooting, editing, and post-production.

7. "Total Domestic Theatrical," which includes Canada, is $10.3 million. Since the theater box

office is $25.5 million, the studio gets only about 40 percent of the box office. This is probably due to the release deal in which theaters reduced the distributor's share after the first two weeks as the price of extending its run. It is also interesting to note that the off-the-top expenses of $32.7 million are more than three times more than the studio's share of the domestic box office (even though it ranked fourth the week it opened).

8. In addition, a $3 million distribution fee was deducted. Warner Bros. could charge a 30 percent fee because it financed the film.

9. The film also lost money on its foreign theatrical distribution, with the expenses of $6 million almost twice the gross. In addition, there is a distribution fee of $1.23 million.

10. The richest profit is the nearly $10 million from US pay-TV. This is a result of an output deal that Warner Bros has with HBO, another Time Warner subsidiary. Note that unlike theatrical release, there are only $308,000 in expenses.

11. Foreign pay-TV of $9.6 million is also the result of Warner Bros. output deals.

12. The domestic video gross of $4.7 million is the 20 percent royalty received from wholesale sales of $23.5 million by Warner Home Video. Warner Home Video retains the balance of $18.8 million to pay the costs of manufacturing and selling the videos, which is probably less than $3 million.

13. The film's total revenues of $52 million were approximately five times the domestic box office. If the domestic and foreign video had been fully accounted for rather than on a royalty basis, the total revenues would have been over $70 million, or seven times the domestic box office.

TO: MIDNIGHT IN THE GARDEN, INCORPORATED
TITLE: MIDNIGHT IN THE GARDEN OF GOOD AND EVIL
RELEASED: NOVEMBER 1997

**WARNER BROS.
ENTERTAINMENT INC.
DISTRIBUTION REPORT NO. 6**

	% FEE	87 MOS ENDED Sep 30, 2007	CUMULATIVE TO DATE
DEFINED GROSS			
Domestic			
Theatrical	30	$783	$10,307,026
Non-Theatrical	30	7,225	275,681
Television	25/35/40	2,161,124	2,174,696
Foreign			
Theatrical/Non-Theatrical	15/35/40	43,392	3,338,227
Television	40	6,663,644	6,688,655
Pay T.V.	30/35/40	6,981,966	23,105,750
Video Cassette	30/35/40	1,489,975	6,347,772
Miscellaneous Royalties	35/40	19,435	19,435
Miscellaneous - Music/Records/Other	0/30	28,205	38,206
Merchandising		0	0
TOTAL DEFINED GROSS		17,395,749	52,295,448
Less: Accounts Receivable		(32,539)	25,612
DEFINED GROSS AFTER ACCOUNTS RECEIVABLE		17,428,288	52,269,836
DISTRIBUTION FEE		6,146,450	17,525,285
DEFINED GROSS AFTER DISTRIBUTION FEE		11,281,838	34,744,551
EXPENSES			
Prints		32,446	3,398,540
Preprint, Dubbing, Subtitles, Editing, etc.		19,834	1,051,971
Advertising and Publicity (includes 10% override)		215,641	33,832,003
Taxes, Duties, Customs and Fees		454,080	875,451
Trade Associations		123	134,933
Freight, Cartage, Handling and Insurance		3,789	481,631
Miscellaneous, Checking and Collection Costs, etc.		4	172,757
Guild, Union and Residual Payments		1,936,866	4,440,200
TOTAL EXPENSES		2,662,783	44,387,486
DEFINED GROSS (LOSS) AFTER DISTRIBUTION FEE AND EXPENSES		8,619,055	(9,642,935)
INVESTMENT AND OTHER			
Negative Cost and/or Advance		870,314	40,654,642
Interest		22,715,783	35,217,886
Gross Participation		0	0
Deferments		0	0
TOTAL INVESTMENT AND OTHER		23,586,097	75,872,528
DEFINED PROCEEDS (DEFICIT)		(14,967,042)	(85,515,463)
Previously Reported		(70,548,421)	
DEFINED PROCEEDS (DEFICIT)		($85,515,463)	($85,515,463)
SHARE OF DEFINED PROCEEDS (3.50%)		$0	$0
AMOUNT ADVANCED		0	0
GUILD RESIDUALS PAID ( )		0	0
PREVIOUSLY PAID			0
(OVERPAID)		0	
		0	0
AMOUNT DUE (DEFICIT)		$0	$0

1 2 3 4 5 6

As a courtesy to you, we are supplying you with this statement showing cumulative figures, upon the understanding, however, that the furnishing of this report shall be without prejudice, and shall not vary or affect in any way the provisions of the agreement between us relating to said picture.

MIDNIGHT IN THE GARDEN
RELEASE # R097629
CONTRACT # 07

LOCATION	DEFINED GROSS	ACCTS REC	DIST FEE	DIST %
CANADA	334,512		100,354	30.00
U.S.A.	9,972,514	155	2,991,708	30.00
TOTAL DOMESTIC THEATRICAL	10,307,026	155	3,092,062	
ARMY/AIR FORCE	14,114		4,234	30.00
INFLIGHT	147,559		44,268	30.00
MISCELLANEOUS U.S. N	6,000		1,800	30.00
NAVY	48,191		14,457	30.00
SWANK	42,607		12,782	30.00
TRANSCOM (DOM.)	17,210		5,163	30.00
TOTAL DOMESTIC NON-THEATRICAL	275,681		82,704	
CAN TV SYND	174,696		69,878	40.00
US NET PRM	2,000,000		500,000	25.00
US TV SYNDI				35.00
TOTAL DOMESTIC FREE TV	2,174,696		569,878	
ARGENTINA	140,207		56,083	40.00
AUSTRALIA	139,167		55,667	40.00
AUSTRIA	15,392		6,157	40.00
BELGIUM	63,785		25,514	40.00
BOLIVIA				40.00
BRAZIL	49,074		19,630	40.00
BULGARIA-F	1,342		201	15.00
CHILE	13,549		5,420	40.00
COLOMBIA-J				15.00
CROATIA	5,902		885	15.00
CYPRUS-LOU	889		133	15.00
CZECH REPU	7,963		3,185	40.00
DENMARK	10,358		4,082	40.00
DOMINICAN	2,000		800	40.00
DUBAI-UAE	30,000		4,500	15.00
ECUADOR				40.00
EGYPT				40.00
ENGLAND	157,493		55,123	35.00
ESTONIA				40.00
FGN UNALLO				40.00
FINLAND	8,405		3,362	40.00
FRANCE	1,158,059		463,224	40.00
GERMANY	54,106		21,642	40.00
GREECE-MIC	27,177		10,871	40.00
HOLLAND	9,666		3,866	40.00
HONG KONG				40.00
HUNGARY	8,763		1,314	15.00
ICELAND-AU	4,091		614	15.00
INDIA				40.00

PRINTS	PREPRINT & EDITING	ADVERTISING & PUBLICITY	TAXES & DUTIES	TRADE ASSOC	FREIGHT	CHECK, COLLECT, & MISC	TOTAL EXPENSES
123,944	44,452	875,926	3,249	3,345	8,292	55	1,059,263
2,364,503	2,287	28,824,523	20,193	99,727	214,031	141,509	31,666,773
2,488,447	46,739	29,700,449	23,442	103,072	222,323	141,564	32,726,036
4,664		3,950					8,614
26,655	5,327	4,079			29		36,090
9,518							9,518
14,615		489					15,104
55,452	5,327	8,518			29		69,326
1,025	99		17,470				18,594
	925	233					1,158
	12,020	18,976					30,996
1,025	13,044	19,209	17,470				50,748
30,917		58,454	22,898	1,402	3,838	2,851	120,360
7,504	5,011	165,912	1,447	1,392	5,149	544	186,959
11,096		23,651	1,958	154	1,010	159	38,028
10,222	26,832	62,126	482	638	4,536	195	105,031
		712	131		263		1,106
51,768	6,872	62,719	11,652	491	7,645	51	141,198
	1,425	2,636	21	13	448		4,543
5,111	15,600	7,526	4,521	135	726	19	33,638
18,954	394	4,246	1,391		1,608		26,593
2,129	1,109	3,244		59	1,100		7,641
516	564	1,367	183	9	554	55	3,248
2,381	6,235	6,422	120	80	1,360	247	16,845
4,507	9,603	23,034	346	103	1,148		38,741
				20			20
	1,030			300			1,330
		3					3
	1,315	744	1,151		1,157	55	4,422
15,817	31,290	418,451	7,195	1,575	19,778	1,544	495,650
	564	956			515	55	2,090
-209,436	11,726	324,534			7,762	10,308	144,894
2,149	11,124	23,505	232	84	2,496		39,590
348,714	240,132	734,723	7,100	11,581	62,260		1,404,510
129,075	109,540	349,014	6,863	541	26,315	7,277	628,625
2,149	5,568	25,697	2,836	272	2,443		38,965
2,930	17,451	191,386	1,675	97	5,156		218,695
2,149	1,069	7,088			66		10,372
2,149	3,516	6,112	148	88	950	133	13,096
	365	3,851		41	1,052		5,309
		363					363

MIDNIGHT IN THE GARDEN
RELEASE # R097629
CONTRACT # 07

LOCATION	DEFINED GROSS	ACCTS REC	DIST FEE	DIST %
INDONESIA				40.00
ISRAEL	28,091		11,236	40.00
ITALY-PIC	128,140		51,256	40.00
JAMAICA			.	40.00
JAPAN	119,109		47,644	40.00
JORDAN-DUN	4,000		600	15.00
KOREA				15.00
LATIN AMER				15.00
LATVIA				40.00
LEBANON	2,390		956	40.00
LITHUANIA				40.00
MALAYSIA	9,087		3,635	40.00
MEXICO	106,134		42,454	40.00
NEW ZEALAN	18,472		2,771	15.00
NORWAY	8,540		3,416	40.00
PANAMA				40.00
PARAGUAY-I				15.00
PERU				40.00
PHILIPPINE	31,326		12,530	40.00
POLAND	10,749		1,640	40.00
PORTUGAL	52,759		21,104	40.00
PUERTO RIC	2,079		832	40.00
ROMANIA-FI				15.00
RUSSIA				15.00
SERBIA				15.00
SINGAPORE	19,491		7,796	40.00
SLOVAKIA	148		59	40.00
SLOVENIA	8,115		1,217	15.00
SO AFRICA	38,260		15,304	40.00
SPAIN-GLOB	530,094	14	211,981	15.00
SWEDEN	18,412		7,365	40.00
SWITZERLAN	57,101		22,840	40.00
TAIWAN	51,802		20,721	40.00
THAILAND	14,286		5,714	40.00
TRINIDAD				40.00
TURKEY	1,271		191	15.00
URUGUAY	3,620		1,448	40.00
VENEZUELA-				40.00
WEST AFRIC	10,414		1,562	15.00
YUGOSLAVIA	3,824		574	15.00
TOTAL FOREIGN THEATRICAL	3,185,102	14	1,239,119	
FGN NON-TH (SUM)	123,005		49,202	40.00
INFLIGHT (FOR)	30,120		12,048	40.00
TOTAL FOREIGN NON-THEATRICAL	153,125		61,250	

9

PRINTS	PREPRINT & EDITING	ADVERTISING & PUBLICITY	TAXES & DUTIES	TRADE ASSOC	FREIGHT	CHECK, COLLECT, & MISC	TOTAL EXPENSES
		606			24		630
2,149	11,230	35,790	1,269	281	2,088		52,807
69,202	111,790	377,233	6,339	1,281	8,997	117	574,959
		979			71		1,050
25,780	21,155	274,626	7,708	1,191	7,882		338,342
				40			40
2,149		5,753	695		950		9,547
	28,415						28,415
	564	902			357	55	1,878
2,149	4,519	1,861	3,321	24	3,042		14,916
					386		386
2,149	2,742	3,270	1,115	91	1,483		10,850
71,648	27	40,018	9,608	1,061	13,612		135,974
2,149	1,619	20,977	749	185	3,037	92	28,808
2,149	18,905	41,414	2,320	85	1,899		66,772
		5,139	465		1,136	50	6,790
500				10	157		667
		1,990	4,749		47		6,786
2,259	1,618	21,744	6,535	313	3,286	1,635	37,390
2,149	8,289	16,608	1,294	107	1,491		29,938
2,369	16,974	30,324	3,417	528	3,787	36	57,435
21,103	277	10,811	437	21	3,073		35,722
1,805	564	1,768	60		1,261	55	5,513
	742	7					749
		41					41
2,307	935	8,760	2,811	195	1,569		16,577
	383	847		1	155	55	1,441
2,149	3,103	2,514		81	1,285		9,132
2,248	4,651	29,443	228	383	4,516		41,469
105,094	95,517	236,853	31,782	5,301	8,760	1,751	485,058
2,149	9,971	63,338	1,387	184	2,482	129	79,640
8,061	17,829	41,886	683	571	4,179		73,209
2,629	19,419	38,979	3,923	518	1,711		67,179
16,339	13,851	13,412	3,020	143	3,204	262	50,231
		1,572	90		437		2,099
2,927		4,015	89	13	305		7,349
		967	1,564	36	60	79	2,706
	388	2,376	480		163		3,407
		1,696	46	104	4,429	31	6,306
	2,763	6,130		38	914		9,845
794,413	906,575	3,853,125	168,534	31,861	251,570	27,840	6,033,918
1,623	2,774	2,535	364		1,256		8,552
1,833							1,833
3,456	2,774	2,535	364		1,256		10,385

MIDNIGHT IN THE GARDEN
RELEASE # R097629
CONTRACT # 07

LOCATION	DEFINED GROSS	ACCTS REC	DIST FEE	DIST %
TOTAL FGN THEAT & NON-THEAT	3,338,227	14	1,300,369	
ALBANIA	800		320	40.00
ANGOLA	450		180	40.00
ARGENTINA	28,372		11,349	40.00
AUSTRALIA	377,068		150,827	40.00
AUSTRIA	54,000		21,600	40.00
BAHRAIN ISL	1,200		480	40.00
BELGIUM	90,914		36,366	40.00
BRAZIL	133,732		53,493	40.00
BULGARIA-FI	7,000		2,800	40.00
CHILE	32,000		12,800	40.00
COLOMBIA	23,000		9,200	40.00
COSTA RICA	3,850		1,540	40.00
CYPRUS-LOUD	4,200		1,680	40.00
CZECH REPUB	59,999		24,000	40.00
DENMARK	30,320		12,128	40.00
DOMINICAN R	1,000		400	40.00
ECUADOR	3,600		1,440	40.00
EL SALVADOR	1,320		528	40.00
ENGLAND	610,616		244,246	40.00
ESTONIA	2,000		800	40.00
ETHIOPIA-NA	650		260	40.00
FGN UNALLOC				40.00
FINLAND	41,001		16,400	40.00
FRANCE	619,192		247,677	40.00
GERMANY	933,913		373,565	40.00
GREECE-MICH	72,907		29,163	40.00
GUATEMALA	1,000		400	40.00
HOLLAND	90,750		36,300	40.00
HONDURAS	1,600		640	40.00
HONG KONG	10,000		4,000	40.00
HUNGARY-FIL	11,500		4,600	40.00
INDONESIA	14,000		5,600	40.00
IRELAND	45,501		18,200	40.00
ISRAEL	30,000		12,000	40.00
ITALY-PIC	1,282,792		513,117	40.00
IVORY COAST	364		146	40.00
JAPAN	400,734		160,294	40.00
JORDAN-DUNI	750		300	40.00
KOREA				40.00
KUWAIT				40.00
LATIN AMERI				40.00
LATVIA	2,143		857	40.00
LEBANON	2,500		1,000	40.00
LITHUANIA	3,500		1,400	40.00
MALAYSIA-GL	5,175		2,070	40.00
MEXICO	30,700		12,280	40.00

PRINTS	PREPRINT & EDITING	ADVERTISING & PUBLICITY	TAXES & DUTIES	TRADE ASSOC	FREIGHT	CHECK, COLLECT, & MISC	TOTAL EXPENSES
797,869	909,349	3,855,660	168,898	31,861	252,826	27,840	6,044,303
710			4,965				5,675
1,452							1,452
			5,400				5,400
167							167
562							562
880			20,061				20,941
			1,051				1,051
230			6,400				6,630
209			5,593		25		5,827
209			771				980
227							227
235			112				347
					80		80
209							209
			119				119
209			264				473
1,064							1,064
167							167
-40							-40
349							349
15,773			247		11	228	16,259
2,564						39	2,603
523			9,081				9,604
209			300				509
488	50				16		554
382			60				442
1,069			164		6		1,239
859							859
579							579
167			2,625				2,792
211	195		102,623				103,029
			73				73
1,233	1,314		9,331		166		12,044
			75				75
436							436
167							167
1,860	15,569						17,429
			214				214
70							70
167							167
			518				518
1,815			3,070		18		4,903

MIDNIGHT IN THE GARDEN
RELEASE # R097629
CONTRACT # 07

LOCATION	DEFINED GROSS	ACCTS REC	DIST FEE	DIST %
MOROCCO	5,712		2,285	40.00
NEW GUINEA,	500		200	40.00
NEW ZEALAND	77,040		30,816	40.00
NICARAGUA	800		320	40.00
NORWAY	26,584		10,634	40.00
PANAMA	4,998		1,999	40.00
PERU	5,000		2,000	40.00
PHILIPPINES	35,000		14,000	40.00
POLAND	128,982		51,593	40.00
PORTUGAL	60,000		24,000	40.00
PUERTO RICO	19,992		7,997	40.00
ROMANIA-FIL	21,001		8,400	40.00
RUSSIA	262,900		105,160	40.00
SAUDI ARABI	10,000		4,000	40.00
SINGAPORE				40.00
SLOVAKIA	9,999		4,000	40.00
SLOVENIA				40.00
SO AFRICA	115,851		46,340	40.00
SPAIN-WHV	607,784		243,114	40.00
SWEDEN	56,643		22,657	40.00
SWITZERLAND	51,173		20,469	40.00
TAIWAN				40.00
THAILAND	20,000		8,000	40.00
TURKEY	40,000		16,000	40.00
TV HOME OFF				40.00
UKRAINE				40.00
URUGUAY	2,901		1,160	40.00
VENEZUELA-E	27,180		10,872	40.00
VIETNAM	1,100		440	40.00
YUGOSLAVIA-	31,402		12,561	40.00
TOTAL FOREIGN FREE TV	**6,688,655**		**2,675,463**	
CANADA	177,485		53,246	30.00
U.S.A.	9,818,053		2,945,416	30.00
TOTAL DOMESTIC PAY TV	**9,995,538**		**2,998,662**	
U.S.A.	3,000,000		900,000	30.00
TOTAL DOMESTIC BASIC CABLE TV	**3,000,000**		**900,000**	
ARGENTINA	5,000		2,000	40.00
AUSTRALIA	158,870		63,548	40.00
BELGIUM	50,630		20,252	40.00
BRAZIL	117,213		46,885	40.00
CHILE	1,000		400	40.00
COLOMBIA	2,797		1,119	40.00
CZECH REPUB	11,133		4,453	40.00

10

PRINTS	PREPRINT & EDITING	ADVERTISING & PUBLICITY	TAXES & DUTIES	TRADE ASSOC	FREIGHT	CHECK, COLLECT, & MISC	TOTAL EXPENSES
			50				50
1,284			2,193		85		3,562
			48		154		202
230			302		11		543
209			300				509
262			3,501				3,763
795			4,898				5,693
23			6,000				6,023
243			5,799				6,042
			2,099				2,099
551							551
			4,500				4,500
664							664
385			306		53		744
200							200
757			7,334				8,091
1,398	2,075		48,623		103	80	52,279
838	749						1,587
230							230
20			1,000				1,020
685							685
3,482	24,801	6,464	211		289	425	35,672
167							167
554			261				815
878			2,039		41		2,958
			110				110
			2,225				2,225
49,266	44,753	6,464	264,916		1,058	772	367,229
		3,424	17,065				20,489
6,435	32,759	238,279	2,500		5,395	2,581	287,949
6,435	32,759	241,703	19,565		5,395	2,581	308,438
46							46
46							46
			875				875
			9,911				9,911
			17,581				17,581
			200				200
			681				681
			800				800

MIDNIGHT IN THE GARDEN
RELEASE # R097629
CONTRACT # 07

LOCATION	DEFINED GROSS	ACCTS REC	DIST FEE	DIST %
ENGLAND	3,869,022		1,354,158	35.00
FIJI	370		148	40.00
FRANCE	857,067		342,827	40.00
GERMANY	573,739		229,496	40.00
GREECE-MICH	86,322		34,529	40.00
HOLLAND	187,080		74,832	40.00
HONG KONG	15,000		6,000	40.00
HUNGARY-FIL	16,000		6,400	40.00
ICELAND-GLO	11,163		4,465	40.00
IRELAND	291		116	40.00
ISRAEL	131,758		52,703	40.00
ITALY-PIC	146,152		58,461	40.00
JAPAN	1,025,266		410,106	40.00
KOREA-KISHI	14,000		5,600	40.00
MEXICO	10,041		4,016	40.00
NEW ZEALAND	78,000		31,200	40.00
POLAND	45,000		18,000	40.00
ROMANIA-FIL	6,628		2,651	40.00
RUSSIA	21,813		8,725	40.00
SAUDI ARABI	22,500		9,000	40.00
SINGAPORE	148,915		59,566	40.00
SO AFRICA	292,073		116,829	40.00
SPAIN	1,059,137		423,655	40.00
SWEDEN	171,802		68,721	40.00
TUNISIA	24,881		9,952	40.00
TURKEY	80,973		32,389	40.00
VENEZUELA-E	350,558		140,223	40.00
TOTAL FOREIGN PAY TV	**9,592,194**		**3,643,425**	
BELGIUM	85,068		34,027	40.00
FRANCE	54,164		21,666	40.00
GERMANY	71,685		28,674	40.00
INDIA	21,101		8,440	40.00
ISRAEL	50,000		20,000	40.00
ITALY-PIC	15,000		6,000	40.00
KOREA-KISHI	24,000		9,600	40.00
MEXICO	19,000		7,600	40.00
RUSSIA	4,999		2,000	40.00
SPAIN	48,500		19,400	40.00
TAIWAN	22,000		8,800	40.00
VENEZUELA-E	102,501		41,000	40.00
TOTAL FOREIGN BASIC CABLE TV	518,018		207,207	
TOTAL DOM & FGN PAY & BSC CABLE	23,105,750		7,749,294	
CANADA	315,073		94,522	30.00

(11)

PRINTS	PREPRINT & EDITING	ADVERTISING & PUBLICITY	TAXES & DUTIES	TRADE ASSOC	FREIGHT	CHECK, COLLECT, & MISC	TOTAL EXPENSES
			46				46
			10,632				10,632
			248				248
			11,797				11,797
			11,692				11,692
			102,526				102,526
			1,004				1,004
			114				114
			663				663
			6,534				6,534
			44,675				44,675
			23,493				23,493
			84,731				84,731
			263				263
			26,877				26,877
			355,343				355,343
			4,375				4,375
			1,200				1,200
			1,650				1,650
			1,900				1,900
			3,880				3,880
			4,400				4,400
			8,412				8,412
			25,817				25,817
6,481	32,759	241,703	400,725		5,395	2,581	689,644

MIDNIGHT IN THE GARDEN
RELEASE # R097629
CONTRACT # 07

LOCATION	DEFINED GROSS	ACCTS REC	DIST FEE	DIST %
U.S.A.	4,414,053	12,650	1,320,421	30.00
TOTAL DOMESTIC VIDEO	**4,729,126**	**12,650**	**1,414,943**	
ARGENTINA	23,398	79	9,328	40.00
AUSTRALIA	131,365	348	52,407	40.00
AUSTRIA	5,233		2,093	40.00
BELGIUM	10,067		4,027	40.00
BENELUX - W	29,265	472	11,517	40.00
BOSNIA	46		18	40.00
BRAZIL	53,667	76	21,436	40.00
BULGARIA-FI	1,290		516	40.00
CHILE	2,906		1,162	40.00
CHINA-MAINL	7,423		2,969	40.00
COLOMBIA	827		331	40.00
CROATIA	9,837		3,935	40.00
CYPRUS-GLOB	25		10	40.00
CZECH REPUB	4,115		1,646	40.00
DENMARK	20,993	2	8,396	40.00
EGYPT	2,020		808	40.00
ENGLAND	193,215	284	67,526	35.00
FINLAND	9,123		3,649	40.00
FRANCE	238,956	9,266	91,876	40.00
GERMANY	84,124	495	33,452	40.00
GREECE-MICH	10,309	5	4,122	40.00
GUATEMALA	1,290		516	40.00
HOLLAND	19,652		7,861	40.00
HONG KONG	8,348		3,339	40.00
HUNGARY-FIL	6,193	378	2,326	40.00
ICELAND	3,417		1,367	40.00
ISRAEL	5,532	62	2,188	40.00
ITALY-PIC	88,977	579	35,359	40.00
JAPAN	234,874		93,950	40.00
JORDAN-DUNI	24		10	40.00
KOREA	22,668		9,067	40.00
KUWAIT	418	8	164	40.00
LEBANON	319		128	40.00
MALAYSIA-GL	547		219	40.00
MEXICO	16,357	161	6,478	40.00
NEW ZEALAND	8,436	84	3,341	40.00
NORWAY	9,918		3,967	40.00
PAKISTAN	523		209	40.00
PARAGUAY	231		92	40.00
PERU	592		237	40.00
PHILIPPINES	6,376	3	2,549	40.00
POLAND-FILM	14,416		5,766	40.00
PORTUGAL	15,054	449	5,842	40.00
ROMANIA-FIL	929		372	40.00
RUSSIA	4,394		1,758	40.00

MIDNIGHT IN THE GARDEN
RELEASE # R097629
CONTRACT # 07

LOCATION	DEFINED GROSS	ACCTS REC	DIST FEE	DIST %
SAUDI ARABI	2,816		1,126	40.00
SERBIA	1,703	10	677	40.00
SINGAPORE	5,596		2,238	40.00
SLOVENIA	20		8	40.00
SO AFRICA-G	16,204		6,482	40.00
SPAIN-WHV	173,889		69,556	40.00
SWEDEN	40,463		16,185	40.00
SWITZERLAND	29,040		11,616	40.00
TAIWAN	21,526		8,610	40.00
THAILAND	9,171		3,668	40.00
TURKEY	3,829	4	1,530	40.00
UNITED ARAB	2,328	24	922	40.00
URUGUAY	2,176	4	869	40.00
VENEZUELA-E	2,196		878	40.00
TOTAL FOREIGN VIDEO	1,618,646	12,793	632,694	
TOTAL DOMESTIC & FOREIGN VIDEO	6,347,772	25,443	2,047,637	
CANADA DOM CPYRT	9,024		3,610	40.00
U.S.A. DOM CPYRT	464		162	35.00
TOTAL DOMESTIC COPYRIGHT	9,488		3,772	
ARGENTINA FGN CPYRT	108		43	40.00
FINLAND AGICOA	219		88	40.00
FRANCE FGN CPYRT	7,755		3,102	40.00
GERMANY FGN CPYRT	273		109	40.00
HOLLAND AGICOA	822		329	40.00
HOLLAND FGN CPYRT	134		54	40.00
ITALY-PIC FGN CPYRT	604		242	40.00
ROMANIA AGICOA	20		8	40.00
SLOVAKIA AGICOA	12		5	40.00
TOTAL FOREIGN COPYRIGHT	9,947		3,980	
TOTAL DOM & FGN COPYRIGHT	19,435		7,752	
U.S.A. INTERNET	421		126	30.00
U.S.A. MUSIC	37,785			
TOTAL MISCELLANEOUS	38,206		126	
TOTAL ALL MEDIA	52,295,448	25,612	17,525,285	

13

ABOUT THE AUTHOR

Edward Jay Epstein studied government at Cornell and Harvard universities and received a Ph.D. from Harvard in 1973. His master's thesis on the search for political truth (*Inquest: The Warren Commission and the Establishment of Truth*) and his doctoral dissertation on television news (*News from Nowhere*) were both published. He taught political science at MIT and UCLA but decided that writing books was a more educational enterprise. *The Hollywood Economist*, which originated as a column on *Slate*, is his fourteenth book. He lives in New York City.

www.edwardjayepstein.com